ALL IN

ALL IN

Gambling on Life, Love, and Faith in a World of Risk

MICHAEL DIMARCO

Revell
Grand Rapids, Michigan

Published by Fleming H. Revell
a division of Baker Publishing Group
P.O. Box 6287, Grand Rapids, MI 49516-6287
www.revellbooks.com

Printed in the United States of America

Library of Congress Cataloging-in-Publication Data
DiMarco, Michael.
    All in : gambling on life, love, and faith in a world of risk / Michael DiMarco.
        p.   cm.
    ISBN 10: 0-8007-1862-3 (cloth)
    ISBN 978-0-8007-1862-6 (cloth)
    1. Risk-taking (Psychology)—Religious aspects—Christianity. I. Title.
BV4598.15.D56 2006
248.4—dc22   2006014973

Published in association with Yates & Yates, LLP, Literary Agents, Orange, California.

The subject of gambling is all encompassing.
It combines man's natural play instinct
with his desire to know about his fate and his future.

Franz Rosenthal

CONTENTS

What happens in Vegas, stays in Vegas
to keep the money you left there company.

Michael DiMarco

wo years into a period of compulsive gambling when I piled up nearly $100K in personal debt and saw my personal life and work ethic spiral into shambles, I found myself staring at a pair of aces. In Texas Hold'em poker, this is the best hand you can have. The only problem was, I was playing blackjack. And after an initial winning streak, I was now losing badly.

In blackjack, the play that any gambler will tell you to make with aces is to split the aces. This means you put out a bet to match your original bet as if you're playing two hands, and the dealer splits the aces and deals one card on top of each, with no option of taking more cards to increase your total. The hope is that you get 10s or face cards (equaling 10) to give yourself 21 on both hands since the ace can equal 11 or 1, whichever benefits the player.

With all my chips on the table already bet on that hand (just shy of the table max of $500), I had one purple $500 chip still hidden in my pocket. That chip represented my insurance policy. It was money that wasn't mine. I had "borrowed" it from work and needed to return it to keep me in the gambling game. For the first time in my degenerate gambling life, I didn't pray to God for a winning hand or a specific card. Instead, I muttered a simple request as I dug for the chip.

"Dear God, get me out of this. I don't care how, just get me out."

The cards were dealt. I made an 18 on one hand and 20 on the other. Not bad. The dealer showed a 7. Usually I'd be visualizing a 10 underneath (for a hand of 17) so that I could automatically win both. But this time I exercised neither mojo nor juju; I just waited to see how God would answer my no-strings-attached prayer. The dealer flipped the hidden card. It was a 9.

"Sixteen," the dealer said, making the move to the shoe to draw a card that should, statistically speaking, bust her hand. A 6 or higher would make her go over 21.

She drew a 5.

"Twenty-one," she said somberly, slowly raking my last thousand dollars into the house's stacks.

What's the difference between a long shot and a sure thing? What makes a person drive fifteen minutes out of their way, pick six or more "lucky" numbers, stand in line for a few minutes, pay $1 for a lottery ticket, and dream for hours about what they would do with the winnings? What keeps that same person from staying at work an extra thirty minutes to finish a project early, or from using that time on a hobby they hope turns into a career they love? And how can we have both the wings to risk and the anchor of procrastination fastened to us at the same time?

The odds of winning the jackpot off of a $1 pick-six lotto ticket are over 49 million to 1; you're 70 times more likely to be hit by lightning. Now that's a long shot. Working late on a project without needing a looming deadline is most likely a sure thing, getting you noticed at work for consistently delivering. So what makes some of us deathly afraid of buying a lotto ticket for fear of becoming addicted while others are fearsome of putting in extra effort at work? Therein lies the hidden mystery of risk.

Have you ever had one of those moments in your life when you felt on top of the world, but soon after you just weren't satisfied and needed more and needed it now? I've had more than my share of those moments come and go. One of the biggest came when I had set a five-year goal of becoming a head volleyball coach at either my alma mater (where I was a student assistant) or another university. I had worked my tail off recruiting, studying offensive and defensive strategies, putting in extra hours in the office and at home, and making myself visible and useful in other areas of the athletic department while working as an otherwise invisible assistant coach of a "non-revenue" sport. Less than two years later, there I was, a freshly announced head coach of my own program, on top of the world and making more money than any other volleyball coach had made at that university.

That example may or may not resonate with you, but surely most of us have set an ambitious goal in life and then met it—or at least come close. (If you haven't, what are you doing wasting time reading a book? Oh, wait, maybe this book will help.) The question is, what did you do next?

After I reached my big goal, something happened: I stopped dreaming big. Well, that's not exactly true. I never stopped *dreaming* big, but I stopped **working** toward my big dreams. Life's best gradually started slipping from a sure thing to a long shot. I started to let my dreams write checks my actions refused to cash. And the only way I could feed that appetite for success without putting in real effort was to start betting on long shots, literally. Whether it was taking a long lunch playing $5 blackjack hands at the nearby casino or taking weekend trips to Vegas playing $500 a hand, I was desperately seeking my place on top of the world again.

Five years later, as I slowly excused myself from the table and left my "insurance policy" in the hands of two split aces, I realized that for the first time I couldn't return in a timely manner the money I had "borrowed" (truly, I hope you're reading that as "stolen") from work—nor could I get out of pawn the video equipment that had been entrusted to me. That week, the jig was up. I was about to get my answer to prayer.

◇◇◇◇◇◇◇◇◇ **WHAT IS PROBLEM GAMBLING?** ◇◇◇◇◇◇◇◇◇

"Problem gambling is gambling behavior which causes disruptions in any major area of life: psychological, physical, social, or vocational. The term 'problem gambling' includes, but is not limited to, the condition known as 'pathological' or 'compulsive' gambling, a progressive addiction characterized by increasing preoccupation with gambling, a need to bet more money more frequently, restlessness or irritability when attempting to stop, 'chasing' losses, and loss of control manifested by continuation of the gambling behavior in spite of mounting, serious, negative consequences."

—National Council on Problem Gambling
(www.ncpgambling.org)

Your Turn to Deal

What are some of the self-destructive things you or a
loved one has done out of desperation?

What are some positive things you can do to end
desperation?

Have you ever lied to yourself or others about something
you were doing that you knew was wrong but couldn't
stop?

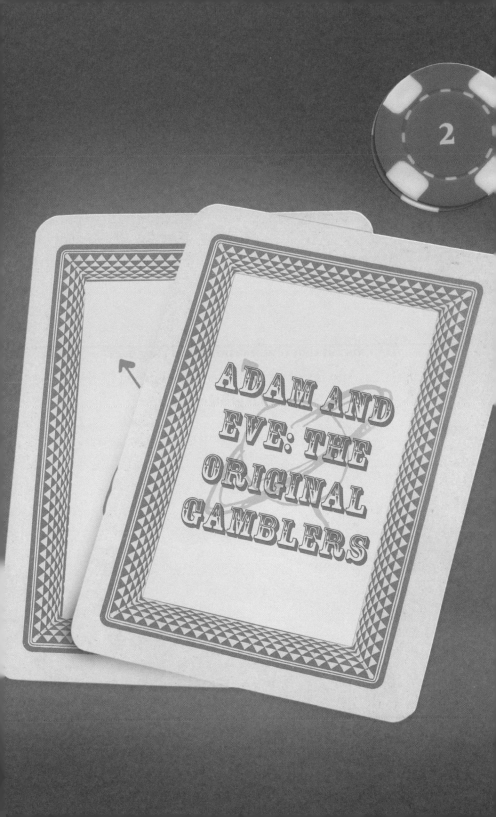

Not all that tempts your wand'ring eyes
And heedless hearts, is lawful prize;
Nor all that glisters, gold.

Thomas Gray, Scottish poet

Right about now I bet you're wondering what happened when I left the table that day. Don't worry. I'll finish my story a little later—otherwise I'll be getting ahead of myself. First we need to go back to the beginning to find the root of the risk problem. And I'm talking *way* back.

From the beginning of time, man has wrestled with risk and the fear associated with it. Ancient tribes on every continent had initiation rituals for men that carried significant risk, at times even death. And most religions point to a genesis moment where man walked with God. But even if you think Adam, Eve, and the Garden of Eden are the stuff of fairy tales, the story provides a first blueprint of assessing risk. The planet's first couple were just given the keys to their dream home when the builder gave them just one instruction.

> But the Lord God gave him this warning: "You may freely eat any fruit in the garden except fruit from the tree of the knowledge of good and evil. If you eat of its fruit, you will surely die."[1]

Unless you just crawled out from under a rock (read Darwin), you know the end of this story. A serpent convinces Eve to eat, and Eve convinces Adam, and the rest is history, literally. God gave the original residents of Eden Vegas a sure thing, but A&E wanted to play slots with the serpent and succumbed to the pull of the invertebrate bandit.

1. Genesis 2:16–17.

One of the interesting things about this story is not the disobedience of the first couple but that God left open to them the option of *thinking about eating the fruit.* Was this loophole a mistake of godly proportions? Or a test where God would follow up with a parental "You knew what I meant"? A calculated pitfall for two creatures purposely created to fall on their faces (and fig leafs)?

In my humble estimation, as Eve started weighing the risks versus the rewards of eating from the tree, she still wasn't disobeying God. Was she mentally careening down a road of epic negative proportions? No question. But there is no disputing the following:

God made us (before original sin) with the capacity to risk and the duty to calculate risk wisely.

Some might call this free will, while others may say it's a disobedient streak. But I truly believe we can see a virtual "risk muscle" in each and every one of us, even going back to before that fateful bite of the apple. Once again, you might not buy the Holy Red Delicious theory, but no one can dispute that every person, culture, and continent on the Earth either embraces or cowers from risk. The fact of the matter is that God required A&E to risk following his one rule. He needed A&E to have faith that the One who created them knew what was best for them and to be obedient to the one rule he had set. Ultimately, faith is taking a risk on things unseen, things empirically unprovable without disobedience. Really, isn't the only way to prove that fruit or a carton of milk has gone bad having someone taste it?

Have you ever reached for milk in your fridge with the intent of drowning your Cheerios, only to find that the date on the top of the container has passed? What do you do in that situation? Throw the milk out immediately? Okay, if it's *way* past date, you probably do throw it out. But what if it's the day of expiration or the day after? I bet you open it and smell it. If the smell doesn't knock you off your feet, you peer into the opening to visually inspect the thickness of Daisy's output. Then, if your data-gathering hasn't ended the pull of your morning ritual, you pour away.

Now, maybe some of you follow expiration dates religiously. My wife, Hayley, is right there with you. Her refrigerator risk level is set to zero. But I bet you, just like her, have no problem exercising your risk muscle in other areas. Keep reading. You risked purchasing this book—I'll sway you yet! To the rest of you, you've just witnessed your risk muscle in action.

God made us (before original sin) with the capacity to measure risk and assign value. And while God established us as creatures capable of weighing risk in our decision making, here is another truth we tend to overlook:

God created us to make those decisions and take those risks without fear.

For those who think the Christian life involves calculating all the ways to avoid risk, excitement, and adventure, check this out. Over and over in the Bible, God is continually telling us to "fear not" and "cast away all fear." But if God doesn't want us to fear, why didn't he just create us without fear in the first place? If we're not supposed to fear, why is it that so many of the risks that we do or don't take are all based around fear? Believe it or not, **God did build us to be fearless**, and all of his reminders to be fearless merely show us just how far we've fallen.

Before my daughter, Addison, arrived on the scene, even before Hayley and I got married, I'd always been a kid magnet. Kids love me (just shows how little they know!). In fact, many of my buddies' kids call me Uncle. How I got Uncle as a nickname is something only my old softball buddies could tell you, but regardless, I always loved seeing new babies enter the world through the homes of my friends when I was single.

I will forever be grateful to my old softball buddy Dan (who still calls me 'Unc' and whose son still calls me Uncle to this day) for two things. But you only get to know one for now.

Dan showed me a trick that provided a major "Aha!" moment for me in raising my own daughter. I don't know if I ever saw this with Dan's firstborn. But when his second-born, Chloe, was about six months old, Dan would cup his hand underneath her feet, and instinctively Chloe would lock her knees and stick her arms out, giggling and shrieking with joy as Dan balanced her on his hand.

I sat on his couch drop-jawed at how much Chloe loved it and how she almost begged for her daddy to keep doing it. Fast-forward the years to a few weeks ago when, over the softest mattress in the house, I decided to gently cup the chunky feet of six-month-old Addison. Just like Chloe years ago, Addy locked up her knees, and immediately she was doing her own balancing act like someone standing on top of a flag pole in midair with the most ecstatic look I had seen yet on her beautiful face. In fact, as soon as I'd swoop her back into my chest, her countenance would drop like a six-year-old driving away from Disneyland.

I have to thank Dan again for that incredible gift. You see, both Chloe and Addy demonstrated that they were completely absent of fear. They were both along for the ride provided by their fathers. And the rides were (and are) pure joy. Regrettably, though, both of our girls are slowly going to be overcome by fear in some way. I think my job as her father, much like our heavenly Father, is to constantly remind her of how it used to be, how it was intended, that she should "fear not" and "cast away all fear." I pray I can reduce fear's effects on Addy, but unfortunately I won't be able to eliminate it completely for her. That's what the knowledge of good and evil brings. It's an open doorway for fear.

Before A&E ate from the tree, they had no concept of fear. Heck, they had no concept of being naked! Check out what happened as they both ate from the tree:

> At that moment, their eyes were opened, and they suddenly felt shame at their nakedness. So they strung fig leaves together around their hips to cover themselves. Toward evening they heard the LORD God walking about in the garden, so they hid themselves among the trees. The LORD God called to Adam, "Where are you?" He replied, "I heard you, so I hid. I was *afraid* because I was naked."[2]

You have just witnessed the first appearance of fear for mankind. One of the hippest trends and coolest phrases of late is to say that "God is calling you to risk." Let me shout this from the mountaintops: the only thing God *ever* asked from us was *obedience*. Risk is an unavoidable aspect of all decision making. But there was a time when we only had one rule: don't eat from the tree of the knowledge of good and evil.

If God's law was tax code, A&E had one box to fill in on the 1040-Eden form—let's say, to pay a 10 percent flat tax. Simple,

2. Genesis 3:7–10, emphasis added.

right? But because they broke that one rule, following God's will and navigating the waters of situational ethics, what is lawful, and what is moral have become instead like memorizing every regulation manual that the IRS publishes. (Everyone is so wrapped up in the "mysterious" *Da Vinci Code*—a work of fiction, by the way—but if you ask me, there are far greater intricacies and mysteries in the tax code!)

During the entire history of the Old Testament, God's people were wandering through the wilderness of decision making. Making choices rarely based on obedience but instead based on fear and self-interest. Instead of being obedient and sticking to a covenant of marriage, God's people asked for tax breaks, loopholes to justify multiple wives, divorce, and the list goes on and on. And still people didn't follow the code.

Of course, the New Testament represents God's effort in tax reform. When the religious leaders of the day sought to trap Jesus with the question "What is the greatest commandment?" he answered with not one rule but two:

Love God with everything you have, and love your neighbor as yourself.[3]

We can't go back to the time of the one-rule society. But we can embrace the revised tax code of these two all-encompassing rules. The genie is out of the bottle, and that genie is fear. That genie is knowledge of the worst-case scenario.

What if my parachute doesn't open?

3. See Mark 12:30–31.

> ◇◇◇◇◇◇◇◇◇◇◇◇◇◇◇◇ **LOVE CONQUERS FEAR** ◇◇◇◇◇◇◇◇◇◇◇◇◇◇◇◇
>
> "Such love has no fear because perfect love expels all fear. If we are afraid, it is for fear of judgment, and this shows that his love has not been perfected in us. We love each other as a result of his loving us first."
>
> 1 John 4:18–19

What if my children end up hating me like I hated my parents?
What if I ask her out and she laughs at me?
What if I fail?

Throughout the history of man, fear has been both a weapon of evildoers and a self-imposed exile that enslaves good people. But if fear enslaves so many, who can enslave fear?

You can.

You can enslave fear in your life by being obedient to God's call to love, by loving him and loving others as yourself. This is one part self-determination and one part dependence. You must determine for yourself that you will become dependent on his love for your assurance that all will turn out right.

The more we love God, the less fear we will have in our lives. Until we trust him and believe that he'll care for us, we'll never rid ourselves of fear. Until I let Addy down in some way (and I'm sure I will), she'll always trust me. That's why Romans 8:28 says, "And we know that God causes everything to work together for the good of those who love God and are called according to his purpose for them."

Maybe it's not so obvious, but loving and valuing others as much as we love and value ourselves dispels fear as well. We only have to look at those who conquer fear daily in service to others (soldiers, police officers, firefighters, missionaries serving lepers) to see that their love for others trumps their fear of danger and death.

Weighing risk is an integral action of decision makers and risk managers everywhere, but fear can be rendered irrelevant if you, like Addy and Chloe, trust your Father's hand. Being obedient to God isn't risky. But the world echoes the words of a certain serpent to convince us that it is. The nutrients of fear from that apple are fused to the DNA of our souls, and fear says obedience is risky. God says, "Enough with the fear—do what is right by others, and trust and follow me."

Your Turn to Deal

Why do you think God didn't say, "Don't even think about eating from the tree of the knowledge of good and evil"?

Can you think of a time when you were "making choices based not on obedience but instead based on fear and self-interest"? Why was that?

What do you think "the nutrients of fear from that apple are fused to the DNA of our souls" means?

If the creator had a purpose in equipping us
with a neck, he surely meant us to stick it out.

Arthur Koestler

nce in a great while, I get a twinge. The itch. I start to crave "action." One thing all gamblers agree on is the love, thrill, and chemical rush of placing a bet. I haven't acted on the urge for a long time, but I still know that I'm addicted to that particular kind of risk. And while I'm going to spend a lot of time attacking fear in *All In*, let's set fear aside for a moment and focus on the issue of risk.

Adam and Eve had two choices in regards to risk in the Garden:

1. Obey God by not eating from the tree and risk missing out on the potential knowledge or experience they could gain by eating the fruit.
2. Eat from the tree and risk missing out on what God had in store for them as obedient children.

One absolute rule of risk: there is no such thing as an absolutely risk-free offer. "Try our product and if you don't like it, return it for a full refund!" What if the company goes out of business or declares bankruptcy? What if you are saddled with paying the shipping and handling charges? What if you forget to return the product within the thirty-day window?

The lesson here is that you can always find risk in any situation. But before we go any further, what is risk exactly?

risk *noun:* a situation involving exposure to danger. *verb:* to act or fail to act in such a way to bring about the possibility of (an unpleasant or unwelcome event)

Oxford American Dictionary

As you can see from the dictionary definitions (both noun and verb), the possibility of an unpleasant event or being exposed to danger are integral to the meaning of risk. I think most of us get that. What's missing from our analysis of the definition of risk is how we define *danger*.

In our book *Marriable: Taking the Desperate Out of Dating* (and its companion books *The Art of Rejection* and *The Art of the First Date*), Hayley and I talk about how so many "nice guys" won't ask girls out on a date because they are paralyzed by the "danger" or "unwelcome event" of rejection. For some reason, having a date, a girlfriend, or even a lifelong soul mate is evidently not worth risking the danger of possibly hearing the word *no*. Meanwhile, these same guys might ride motorcycles, travel to third-world countries for missions or humanitarian reasons, or have a diet that consists solely of fast food. Talk about McRisky!

Here is a list of things I viewed as risky at some point in my life:

Swimming in water where I couldn't touch bottom
Roller coasters
Asking girls out
Breaking up with girls

Hard 16: A blackjack term meaning two or more cards totaling a count of 16. ("Hitting" means asking for another card from the dealer. Since the object of blackjack is to beat the dealer's hand without going over 21, any card in the deck over a 5 will cause the player to bust and lose the hand.)

Going to college

Saving money

Working hard

Hitting a hard 16

Getting married

Getting married again

Getting pregnant (not me, my wife)

Telling the truth

Becoming a man of character

Getting projects done on time

Now, some of the things I have on my list as risky probably don't seem risky to you, like saving money. While others like getting married or divorced do (more on those later). But once again, this has nothing to do with how we define risk but rather has to do with

how we define danger. No one needs help defining risk because the dictionary definition is so clear. It's the way we define what is dangerous to us that creates the different categories of risk in our lives.

People who aggressively immerse themselves in risk with apparent disregard for fear usually fall into one of two categories:

1. Those who seek action
2. Those who seek escape

You can find both action and escape jumping out of an airplane (extreme escape doesn't even require a parachute!). Many vices like drinking or gambling start out as seeking action, but when the addiction hits, they're used more as an escape.

Why do we risk?

For the high.

For a payoff.

To fulfill a duty.

To numb the pain.

And even when we choose to avoid risk in one area of life, we automatically engage in an opposite action of risk by default. Let me explain.

Let's say you're single and in a relationship where you're not happy. But you're afraid that if you break things off, you'll hate being alone. By avoiding the risk of being alone for a time now, you're running the risk of missing out on a more fulfilling relationship.

Likewise, let's suppose you're in a marriage and both of you are unhappy. Things aren't going well, and your spouse is starting D-word rumblings. One of you might be willing to risk rejection and personal

GAMBLERS GONE WILD:
ACTION VS. ESCAPE GAMBLERS

◇◇◇◇◇◇◇◇◇◇◇◇◇◇◇ **GAMBLERS GONE WILD:** ◇◇◇◇◇◇◇◇◇◇◇◇◇◇
◇◇◇◇◇◇◇◇◇◇◇ **ACTION VS. ESCAPE GAMBLERS** ◇◇◇◇◇◇◇◇◇◇◇

"Action gamblers, highly competitive and easily bored, tend to take unnecessary risks and make impulsive decisions. They often prefer poker and blackjack, horse races, professional and college sports, and stock market speculation—where they can exercise some skill, or at least the appearance of skill. Escape gamblers are more likely to play passive games of pure chance—slot machines, bingo, and lotteries. They are often depressed or anxious and use gambling to numb or cheer themselves."

—Harvard Mental Health Letter, March 2004

blame to spend a ton of time on marriage counseling and personal growth in order to fulfill your duty to "love, honor, and cherish, for better or worse." Meanwhile, the other is willing to risk the baggage and hurt that comes with divorce for the payoff of being happier or to numb the pain that the relationship has brought.

For better or worse, when most people assess risk they always ask the question, "What's in it for me?" Instead, the first question that really *should* be asked when weighing risk is, "What is morally right?" Once that question is answered, the second question is, "Is this selfish or good for others?" In other words, does the decision that I want to make only benefit me? Then lastly, "What am I afraid of?" Many times this is the "worst-case scenario."

Have you ever noticed that when analyzing risk and fears during the decision-making process, we always come up with the best-case

scenario and the worst-case scenario but rarely have in mind the myriad of scenarios that lie in between? By default, then, we set up in our minds with "fear math" that we have a 50-50 chance of the worst-case scenario coming to pass. Of course, this works in reverse as well. The eternal optimist thinks his chance of the ultimate positive result is at least 50 percent as well.

In the coming chapters, we'll be exploring the right way to calculate the odds, when to place your bets, and how to win big in the game of life. So let's shuffle up and deal!

Your Turn to Deal

What are some things that you currently consider risky?

What are some things that you used to consider risky?
  What changed?

Are you more likely to risk for action or for escape?
  Why?

What do you think is meant by "fear math"?

No snowflake in an avalanche ever feels responsible.

Stanislaw Lec

Growing up in the Pacific Northwest, every Saturday afternoon I would watch with my dad what he called "spaghetti westerns." Since he was first-generation Italian-American (my Yankee dago daddy), I figured that was some sort of code. Two of our favorite shows were *Maverick* and *Wild Wild West*. Not the ones starring Mel Gibson or Will Smith. The originals. And what was the heroes' game of choice? Poker, of course. They were gamblers.

My father also shared another of his loves with me, although it was a strange one to share with an eight-year-old. He loved studying the founding fathers and in particular reading the Federalist Papers. I think I was the only fourth grader with my own personal copy at school. If only he were alive today to see me blend his two loves in this chapter!

While every country has a time in its history when its citizens took extraordinary risks, the United States is truly a country founded by gamblers. Families crossed the stormy Atlantic to the New World for religious freedom. Wealthy land owners and honorable men risked losing everything in a war to become "founding fathers."

How to Risk in a Powdered Wig:
"We mutually pledge to each other our Lives,
our Fortunes and our sacred Honor."

—The Declaration of Independence

Completely sane people left the safety of the original thirteen colonies to stake a claim in the Wild West when the Wild West was Missouri! And if that wasn't enough, more gambling huddled masses poured into the land of opportunity from all over the world during the twentieth century—including my paternal grandparents, who came from Italy in the early 1900s.

In fact, my grandparents were a great case study on risk. My grandfather, single at the time of his crossing the Atlantic, saw a young woman on the ship who caught his eye. So he took the risk of approaching the girl's father . . . to ask for her hand in marriage.

The hand of a girl he had just seen for the first time.

And hadn't spoken to.

Ever.

For all he knew, she had an annoying laugh or a hot temper. Then again, what Italian woman *doesn't* have a hot temper?

Back in simpler times, though, the reward of marriage and having a helpmate was far greater than the risk of "not being compatible." Compatibility is a requirement for a person feeling *happy* all the time, not for staying married. The only requirement in a mate for staying married is an agreement not to divorce, which is already in the wedding vows! But I digress—back to the story.

When my grandfather Eduardo approached the girl's father and asked for her hand in marriage, the father asked the customary questions you'd expect him to ask when approached by a total stranger wanting him to hand over one of his most priceless treasures.

"Where did you grow up?"

"Who do you know in the States?"

"What are your plans?"

"How much money do you have?"

Satisfied by my grandfather's answers to all of the above, the father agreed to let him marry his daughter and moved to introduce the two. Remember that this is all transpiring on the deck of some ship bobbing in the middle of the Atlantic!

"Louisa!" the father bellowed. A woman not as young as my grandfather had hoped strolled over to meet him. "This is Eduardo DiMarco. He's going to be your husband." My grandfather stammered, "But I thought *she* was your daughter!" pointing to a younger girl near the rail. The father smiled and said, "Oh, she is my daughter too, but Louisa is my oldest. You can marry *her*." My grandfather, in that frozen moment in time, looked Louisa up and down, shrugged his shoulders, and said, "Eh," with an affirmative yet slightly resigned tone. Ah, the romance! They were married, and yes, Louisa had a temper.

What was the biggest gamble my grandfather made? Was it crossing the Atlantic on his own to immigrate to a land he had never seen? Was it asking a woman to marry him whom he had never met? I would love to ask him, but he's long since left this earth. But in this age of conversation about illegal immigration and border security, I would just like to say this: my grandfather came to this

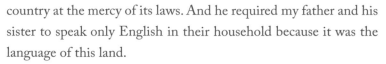

country at the mercy of its laws. And he required my father and his sister to speak only English in their household because it was the language of this land.

For my grandfather, risking his integrity to immigrate illegally wasn't worth the payoff of a speedier assimilation into this country. He associated speaking Italian with the opportunities (and lack thereof) he left in Italy, while he saw risking embarrassment speaking broken English embracing his budding citizenship and belonging in the land of opportunity. (Besides, he could save Italian for all his favorite swear words.)

I use the example of immigration not only because it's become a hot-button issue but also because it demonstrates perfectly how we as humans can lie to ourselves regarding risk. Many will say, "Look at those immigrants digging tunnels, climbing fences, and risking their lives in the desert for their dreams of a better life despite the risk of getting arrested or dying in the process." But remember again the first question to ask when weighing the risk: "Is it morally right?" Likewise, legal residents and citizens are faced with the moral question, "Is it morally right to deport 11 million peaceful people looking for a better life?" A history of civil rights shows that just because a law is on the books doesn't inherently make it morally right. "Who Would Jesus Deport?" is a tough question indeed.

When we abandon our morals and honor in favor of what makes us feel the best the soonest (sneaking over borders/shipping everyone out), we begin to take all the wrong risks for all the wrong reasons because of the fear that we won't get what we want or what we think we deserve. And that gets us into even bigger trouble.

Your Turn to Deal

Is there anything in your life worth giving up everything
to save or protect?

Do you think most people could make a marriage last if
they had only met their spouse once? How about you?
Why do you think things were different back then?

Do you agree that a noble goal or outcome that's based
on an immoral act is a bad decision? Why? Are there
exceptions?

Forget the self and you will fear nothing.

Carlos Castaneda

In poker, if you play scared, other players will smell your fear. If a bead of sweat forms on your forehead or on your upper lip, you might as well fold or just give your opponent your chips, because the game is over. Poker is the only game in which hiding your emotions and even lying is a valuable skill. Such an honorable sport, eh?

If you're not willing to bluff in poker, you become predictable; everyone knows when you have a good hand because that's when you bet. Deception is key in a game of incomplete information, and fear is not an option. If a poker player loses his nerve, he's basically giving himself permission to be afraid even though he knows in his heart that fear will sink his chances in the end.

What is your first memory of an event in your life when you gave yourself permission not to risk—even when every point of reference and a trusted voice told you to take the risk? Did it have to do with not trying a food at the dinner table that the rest of your family loved? Was it not petting the neighbor's dog when the sweet old lady insisted to you that Baxter was friendly?

One of the few memories that stands out from my childhood was a result of my family's summer tradition of all the kids taking swimming lessons. Since I was the youngest of six kids, this was a long-standing tradition, and the local parks and recreation district had a huge indoor pool where we went for weekly lessons during summer break. In your first summer of lessons, you would sit on the side of the wading pool and kick your legs and then progress to the point of floating with a kickboard. Upon graduation you received a "Guppy" ID card stating that you had completed the course. This card would immediately go into my Velcro nylon wallet (every five-year-old needed a Velcro wallet).

The following year was Dolphin class, where the requisite skill at the end was opening your eyes underwater and floating on your back for ten seconds. I remember asking why it wasn't called the Otter class. It's not like we learned a new language of clicking and squealing while jumping through hoops. (Yes, I was a pain in the Anemone then too.) Make that one more card for the wallet. In year three, it was time to become a Shark.

Learning to be a Shark involved a run-of-the-mill crawl or freestyle stroke, preferably with your head down with head-turns to breathe, but you were allowed to keep your head up the whole time as well. Since I wasn't a fan of having my face in the water, I took the accepted half crawl, half dog paddle route. When it came time for the graduation test, our esteemed instructor (looking back, I realize the girl was probably about fourteen) told us aspiring Sharks that we had to move out of the 2- to 4-foot-deep side of the pool into the 5-foot-deep lap swim area and swim one lap, down and back, to get our card.

I froze. My brain raced.

Can't touch bottom?

What happens if I need to?

What happens if I get tired?

I'd hated the one time I accidentally inhaled chlorinated pool water into my nose while diving for a cut piece of garden hose in

BLUFFING

A bluff is simply betting on a hand that you would normally fold because it has a statistically low chance of winning. You are basically risking your chips hoping the other players will fold.

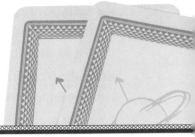

the shallow end, but at least I was able to touch bottom and rocket out of the water like a submarine-launched missile. Or dolphin?

I approached my wise old instructor and asked, "Do I *have* to take the test?"

"If you want to be a Shark you do," she replied.

"That's okay, I'll just be a Dolphin till next year." When faced with a decision to risk facing my fear, instead of moving all in and walking over to the deep end of the pool, I simply folded.

And so began my fear of water, of the high dive, even of roller coasters at the county fair. Anything where I could easily picture my catastrophic demise. If I could picture it happening, I feared it. That day I gave myself permission to not keep up with the rest of the swim class. More importantly, I learned how to give myself permission to try to avoid all risk if at all possible.

It wasn't until after high school that I heard the story of Peter attempting to walk on water with Jesus. In the twenty or so years since first hearing the story, I've heard numerous lessons taught on Peter's faith and sudden loss of faith. Personally, I've always thought it was interesting that Peter didn't appear very awestruck and instead basically raised his hand like Horshack, saying, "Oooh, oooh, I want to do that!" The simple lesson I took from that story back then was Jesus saying, "Look, I'm God, you're not. Believe me now?"

Only recently did I start thinking about the risks and fears Peter had to face *before* he stepped out of the boat.

"That *is* Jesus out there, right?"

"Who am I to think I should be able to ask this?"

"What are the rest of the guys going to think of me asking?"

"When, exactly, will someone invent a lifesaving flotation device?"

"Why hasn't someone cast David Hasselhoff in a biblical role with that hair of his?"

Okay, that last one was mine. And very possibly all of those were mine and none were Peter's. The truth is, we see no fear from Peter until he stepped out on the water. Just the act of asking Jesus if he could join him on the water was a risk.

But his fearful thoughts became evident when he looked down and foresaw a worst-case scenario in his mind. He ignored a trusted voice, and even instantaneous firsthand experience, and slipped on the concrete sandals of fear that dragged him back down to Earth (or at least the waters thereof).

Risk is oftentimes what you measure and think about *before* you step out of the boat and not what you think about while you're on the waves. Fear is what keeps you in the boat and what you allow in your mind during an impossible feat even though you've proved it possible.

I believe that there was no way that Peter could walk all the way out to meet Jesus in this story. Peter would have needed not just extraordinary faith but faith of God-like proportions. And that's the point. Peter wasn't God. I think Jesus surely knew Peter couldn't make it to him and saw an object lesson in the making. Even though Peter had enough faith to risk asking, enough faith to risk accepting, and enough faith to risk walking, he ran out of faith during what I suggest was the least risky part. It's what coaches and athletes say when they give a game away: "We had it won. They didn't beat us; we beat ourselves."

Our family just bought a boat this year, and though our six-month-old is not yet ready to wakeboard, I know that I will be

the one she looks to for that trusted voice when it comes time to face the fear of water and confront her own decisions of risk. I can only pray that I provide enough inspiration and trust that when she sits on the stern of our boat, she won't hesitate to jump *All In.*

Your Turn to Deal

What childhood fear(s) can you remember having
   trouble facing?

Did you face them, and if so, how did you conquer them?
   How did it feel?

When was the last time you gave yourself permission not
   to risk? Why?

All life is the management of risk, not its elimination.

Walter Wriston

Professional gamblers know which games in the casino have the best odds. That's why I played blackjack and craps—because in most variations, you have a greater likelihood of winning over time than in other table games. Here is one of the rare times I'll tell a "positive" gambling story . . . and it *still* doesn't turn out well.

I once walked into a small casino and changed in $400 for chips at a $25 minimum bet blackjack table. After two hours I had won around $3,000. In a playful, half-joking tone, I asked one of the pit bosses how much I could win at the table without the casino reporting it to the IRS. He grinned and told me $9,999.99. I don't know if he was grinning because he thought it was funny or because he knew the odds of me giving back all those chips in front of me were extremely good after that comment. Probably both.

Over the course of the next four hours, I played at that same table until the clock hit 5:00 p.m. (I think I'd called into work "sick" that day.) After tipping the dealer a $500 chip, I walked over to the cashier's window and cashed out for $9,400.

Unfortunately, this was early in my gambling "career" (read: sickness), so I walked out to my car feeling like I could do this once a month if I wanted to. I spent the next two years digging myself toward a deeper and deeper "bottom" until I actually hit it and started my climb back out.

◇◇◇◇◇◇ THE ULTIMATE SURE THING: "THE NUTS" ◇◇◇◇◇◇

One of the strangest terms in poker is when someone says they're holding "the nuts." When you hold the nuts in poker, it means you have an unbeatable hand. If a Hold'em table shows the community cards Kh-8h-3d-2h-Qs and you hold the Ah-9h, then you are holding the nuts, specifically a nut flush. Your two hearts combined with the three on the table give you a flush, and since you hold the ace, no other flush or hand can beat it.

This poker term predates ESPN and *Celebrity Poker Showdown*, going back to the Wild West where poker was the game of choice for cowpunchers and city slickers alike. Whether it was around a campfire, in a bunkhouse, or in a saloon of ill repute, men would wager almost anything of value, all the way up to their horse and wagon. Legend has it that when a cowboy bet his wagon, he would unscrew the lug nuts from his wheels and place them in the pot to insure he couldn't hightail it out of there if he lost the hand. The mere action of betting the nuts to his wagon meant that his hand was a sure thing (or a reckless stone cold bluff).

While my addiction to gambling was less about money than about my emotions and looking to numb pain in my life, for many people, gambling in casinos or playing the lottery *is* about money. Think about this, though: what if I gambled with $100 for one hour a week, and after 60 minutes I left the casino—up, down, or busted—and put the money in a mattress. How much money would I have after ten years? We can't be sure, can we? Knowing me, I'd have zero.

Now say I took the same $100 a week and stuffed it in the mattress right away. We know exactly how much money I'd have after ten years: $52,000. Put that into a 3 percent savings account and I'd have over $61,000. A solid growth mutual fund with a rate of 12 percent? Glad you asked! How does $102,000 sound? Will you wet your pants if I tell you that in twenty years it would be almost a half a million bucks?

Gambling is sexy. Saving is not. At least that's what we tell ourselves. But which of these is more sexy: broke people or rich people? By the way, for anyone out there reading this saying, "All this talk about money is so shallow and temporary in God's eyes," I'd like to point out that hiding money in a mattress versus wise investing parallels a little story called the parable of the talents.[1]

---

1. See Matthew 25:14–30.

◇◇◇◇◇◇◇◇◇◇◇◇◇◇ **PERCEPTION IS REALITY** ◇◇◇◇◇◇◇◇◇◇◇◇◇◇

In the milk carton analogy, I mentioned that my wife, Hayley, is afraid of passing expiration dates. She just doesn't see the need to risk offending her sense of taste or her health by downing two-week-old milk or two-year-old vitamins. But this risk-averse woman is the same girl who in her twenties traveled to Europe and India by herself for over a year.

The real story here is that you can be a risk-taker in one area of your life and refuse to even entertain the thought of risk in others. A bungee jumper who fears opening his heart in relationships. A woman who provides counseling at a juvenile detention facility with no guards present yet can't risk mending fences with an estranged parent. We all have our sweet spots and blind spots when it comes to risk.

Which seems riskier to you: jumping out of an airplane to skydive or commuting to work? Would it surprise you if I told you you'd have to jump 17 times in a year before your odds of dying in a skydiving accident equaled your odds of dying in a car crash? In a research publication from Texas A&M University, Gene Charleton writes:

> So why do so many people consider skydivers to be danger junkies while these same people happily risk their lives on the way to the office? People's perceptions of what is risky and what is not are colored by how they see themselves in relation to the risk. Factors that affect their perceptions include:
>
> • Catastrophic potential—people are more concerned about deaths and injuries that happen all at once (airplane crashes) than they are about those that are scattered (automobile accidents);

- Familiarity—people are more concerned about risks they know little about (ozone depletion) than risks they experience often (household accidents);
- Understanding—people worry more about phenomena they don't understand (radiation exposure) than ones they do (slipping on icy sidewalks);
- Uncertainty—people are more concerned about risks scientists disagree about (recombinant DNA) than risks scientists agree about (auto accidents);
- Control—people are less willing to take risks they feel they can't control (commercial air travel) than ones they feel they do control (driving in heavy traffic);
- Impact on children—people are more concerned about risks that appear to threaten children more than adults;
- Dread—people are more concerned about risks that have terrifying results ("flesh-eating bacteria").[2]

Any of those strike a nerve? I hope so, because when you can identify the fear or blind spot associated with different types of risk, you're halfway home to focusing on real outcomes instead of fear-based fiction. In the coming chapters, we're going to look at various categories of risk and their corresponding fears and break down each one.

2. Gene Charleton, *Advance,* 6th ed., Office of the VPR, Texas A&M University, 2005.

Gambling and using debt to leverage wealth are long shots for creating wealth. Saving and investing tend to be sure things. But you don't have to take my word for it. Read a book like *The Total Money Makeover* by Dave Ramsey or listen to his radio talk show. You'll hear thousands of callers who are consistently paying what he endearingly calls "stupid tax." Many people routinely fail to consider the risks they are taking with money, and in the absence of a moral foundation, they are completely tuned to the long shot behavior of "I want it now!"

Real life is no different than in the casino. A sure thing tends to pay small amounts, so it takes a long time to accumulate wealth or skill, but nearly anyone can do it. A long shot promises a big payday, with a near impossibility of accumulating wealth except for an extremely lucky few. Examining how you "bet" your time and money will show if you're living the life of a long shot or sure thing.

Your Turn to Deal

In the past, what long shots and sure things have you
pursued in your life? How did they turn out?

Why is it that people give up on sure things and spend
time dreaming about the long shot?

What is one long shot you commit to stop obsessing
about or one sure thing that you commit to pursuing
in your life today?

65

One person with a belief is equal to a force
of ninety-nine who only have an interest.

John Stuart Mill

It might seem silly, but I miss having chips in my hands. Tune in to any poker program on TV, and you'll see the players constantly fidgeting with their stacks of chips. Part of this comes from a player's nervous tics and the monotony between hands waiting for action. But a very practical side of doting on your stack is money management.

Back in my "prime" as a compulsive gambler, I would set financial goals of how much I wanted to win off of the house before leaving the casino. At first these goals were set around what toys or luxuries I wanted to add to my life. In the later stages, I would set goals of using my winnings to pay off my student loans, payday loans, or mortgage. There were days when I would literally walk into the local casino at 11 a.m. and close the place down at 1 a.m. Needless to say I would see a lot of hands and make a ton of wagers in one sitting, and in those longer sessions it was easy to lose track of how much I was up or down.

All gamblers will tell you that knowing when to bet big and when to pull back your chips is crucial for staying in the game. Every day we all have to decide how much time, effort, money, and reputation we're going to put into each and every decision we make. Living your life all in doesn't mean risking everything you have on every little decision. It merely means knowing when to bet, what to bet, and how big to bet.

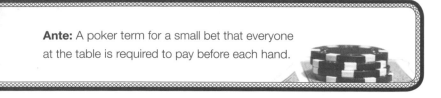

Ante: A poker term for a small bet that everyone at the table is required to pay before each hand.

In a typical casino, the chips are all the same size and weight. Only the color and denomination markings are different. White chips are usually worth $1, red chips are $5, green $25, black $100, purple $500, and so on. In life, our chips might look like this:

White = our attention

Red = our interest

Green = our time

Black = our money

Purple = our reputation

A woman who approaches you in a shopping mall parking lot and says, "Excuse me," is asking you to ante a white chip of attention and bet a red chip of interest. Her sharing, "I'm having some car troubles," asks you to bet a few more interest chips and one green chip of your time.

"I just ran out of gas and I forgot my wallet" says you'll be needing to decide if you'll wager any black chips by giving her money you may never get back. And finally, if you're a married man, her request of "Will you give me a lift back to my apartment?" potentially stakes your reputation on the line.

You have to decide on what and whom you are going to bet your time, effort, and resources—and even what value you give to your various chips. Is your time worth more than your reputation? Your money? Do you proclaim you believe in a surefire betting system but wager your chips in a way that contradicts that?

For instance, do you say sexual purity is part of your belief system but look at porn on the Internet three nights a week? In casino terms, a gambler might say that he never splits face cards, but he'll still tend to do it in the heat of the moment.

In gambling, once you've made the moral justification for *entering* the casino (unless you're just there for the food and Celine Dion concert), you don't think about the moral issues between placing a $5 bet and placing a $25 bet. But in every decision in life, whether it's a split-second decision or one you agonize about over the course of weeks, every "yes" or "no" is betting your interest, attention, time, money, and reputation. And first asking the ethical question "Is it moral?" is something we all do according to our personally accepted standards of conduct.

What is your ethical and moral blueprint? Is it how you were raised? Is it based on the situation, with no black-and-white answers? Is it based on a political party or organizational affiliation? Do you go back in history to a philosopher or religious text? For me and my house, our ethical standard is the Bible. That's basically our betting system. We're betting that our ethical standard is going to help us win in life. You may have a betting system too. And you're betting your personal chips won't be wasted and you'll be able to build huge stacks of attention, interest, time, wealth, and/or reputation—any combination of those resources, depending on what your ethical system values.

Consider the following a crash course on ethics. I promise it won't hurt, there won't be a test, and it just might help you better

Splitting face cards (or 10s): A blackjack term. Since the object of the game is to get as close to 21 as possible without going over ("busting"), if a player is dealt two 10s or two face cards (whose value is also 10), the player has 20, the second best hand in blackjack. The rules allow the player to split two cards of equal value into two separate hands, with each card representing the first card in the hand with the second and subsequent cards to be dealt by the dealer. A second matching bet is needed for the second hand, thus doubling the money wagered and putting twice as much at risk while deconstructing the second best hand in the game.

understand how you and others might value your chips. The Mark-kula Center for Applied Ethics at Santa Clara University identifies five ethical approaches from which moral standards (or your life's betting rules) come.[1]

The Utilitarian Approach. Basically this says that an ethical action is the one that does the most good or

1. Paraphrased from http://www.scu.edu/ethics/practicing/decision/framework.html.

the least harm to the most people. It deals heavily with consequences, trying to increase the good and to reduce the harm as much as possible.

The Rights Approach. Other philosophers and ethicists say that the most ethical action is the one that best protects and respects the *moral* rights of those affected. This approach argues that people have a right to be treated as ends and not merely as means to other ends. This includes things like the rights to make your own choices about what kind of life to lead, to be told the truth, to not be injured, to have a degree of privacy, and so on.

The Fairness or Justice Approach. Aristotle and other Greek philosophers contributed the idea that all equals should be treated equally, which has come to mean we treat everyone equally. We pay people more based on their harder work or the greater amount that they contribute to an organization, and we say that is fair. But CEO salaries that are hundreds of times larger than the pay of others are now being debated; many ask whether the huge disparity is based on a defensible standard or is the result of an imbalance of power and hence is unfair.

The Common Good Approach. The Greek philosophers have also contributed to the idea that community is a good in itself and all our actions should contribute to community. They reason that respect and compassion for all others, especially

the vulnerable, are required. This approach also
calls attention to the common conditions that are
important to the welfare of everyone. This may be a
system of laws, effective police and fire departments,
health care, a public educational system, or even
public recreational areas.

The Virtue Approach. A very ancient approach to
ethics is that ethical actions ought to be consistent
with certain ideal virtues. These virtues help us to act
according to the highest potential of our character
and on behalf of values like truth and beauty. Honesty,
courage, compassion, generosity, tolerance, love,
fidelity, integrity, fairness, self-control, and prudence
are all examples of virtues. Virtue ethics asks of any
action, "What kind of person will I become if I do
this?" or "Is this action consistent with my acting at
my best?"

While ethicists separate ethical approaches into these five categories, it's fascinating that the principles of all five are interwoven throughout the Bible. In the virtue approach, the questions "What kind of person will I become if I do this?" and "Is this action consistent with my acting at my best?" could also be reworded as "Will this help me to become the person God wants me to be?" and "Will God be pleased with how my decision impacts others?"

Interestingly, these questions line up with one the Pharisees asked Jesus: "What is the greatest commandment?" In other words, what is your greatest single ethical standard? Or in gambling terms, "What's your betting system for life?" Jesus gave them life's formula for breaking the bank: love God and love others as yourself.

Now that we've identified what our chips are and looked at the ethical standards that assign them value, it's time to put our betting strategy into action.

The wicked flee when no one pursues,
but the righteous are bold as a lion.

Proverbs 28:1 English Standard Version

All In translation:
Courage is only found in a person
with moral character. Cowardice should
only be found in the wicked
or the spiritually dead.

Your Turn to Deal

Try to remember the last time a stranger tried to get your
attention for help or vice versa. Were they/you able to
grab the other person's interest? What happened? Did
you/they help?

Which ethical approach most sounded like the way
you weigh morality? Why is it important to have a
standard?

Of the "values chips" mentioned (time, money, reputation,
etc.), which do you wish you had more of? Why?

A WINNING SYSTEM

It is easier to fight for one's principles
than to live up to them.

Alfred Adler

When you grow up the youngest of six in an Italian-Irish family, you compete for two things: food and attention. And while food was sparse at times during my childhood, I found what I thought was a winning system to get my parents' attention (and everyone else's for that matter). If I could make people laugh or give them the answer I thought they wanted to hear, I knew that I could win in life. That was the system or approach on life that was the foundation for everything I said or did. And since this system had no moral foundation or higher authority, my approach to life was all about me.

Life in the casino is no different. Each citizen of Slot City has a system. If I had a dollar for every blackjack approach, craps strategy, poker philosophy, or slots system circulating the Internet and cluttering the gaming section at the local bookstore, I'd have enough money to open a casino and take all their devotees' money! Not that I'd do such a thing, of course.

While there is no guaranteed system to avoid losing in a casino except for not going into one, I have found a winning system for decision making in life. Make sure you understand—I didn't invent this system, *I found it*.

Truth can't be invented; it can merely be found and brought to the surface. There are a lot of variations of this system out there, and

I cannot agree with those who say that
they have 'new truth' to teach. The
two words seem to me to contradict
each other; that which is new is not
true. It is the old that is true, for truth
is as old as God himself.

Charles Spurgeon

this is just one ex-gambler's take on a five-step system for decision-making when risk is involved.

Character before Action

Impossible to gain overnight, character is something that you must develop as a man or woman of God in order to make good decisions. Jesus himself said in the Sermon on the Mount that character comes before conduct and that moral character is something that is inside you before it's seen by others.[1] When we have character, we possess an inner moral compass that molds our identity into a predictable one, and it's these attributes of virtue that gives us peace in doing the right thing and the backbone to resist temptation.

Make Facts Your Friends

Listening and asking the right questions are the tools of a good decision-maker. Questions surrounding the situation and the people involved and an honest evaluation of your own abilities and character should all factor into making a godly response. Sometimes facts can be killjoys, killing your decision before it starts and taking away the option of what you *wish* you could do. This is a good thing. Let facts have your back.

Open the Rulebook

We've got character and the facts (at least what we could come up with to this point), so now we have to answer any ethical questions

1. See Matthew 5–7.

that might be involved. They may help us to move forward or may preempt or redirect our current decision-making path. Broad ethical standards are found in the Ten Commandments[2] and the Sermon on the Mount.[3] For individual virtues like love, justice, and servant-hood, we can look to places like Matthew 22:36–40, 1 Corinthians 13, Amos 5:24, and Matthew 20:26–28.

No system or its steps are without interpretation, and this step is no exception. Deciding to choose the greater good or the lesser evil may be a choice you're faced with when deciding between two conflicting values like love and truth. Every husband and boyfriend in the known world recognizes the inherent conflict in responding to the question, "Does this make me look fat?"

Count the Cost

Whether the motivation is selfless or selfish, everyone wants to know how the outcome is going to potentially affect them and others. This is an important step in making moral choices—asking, "Does this bring good to others?" Notice that we didn't start our process with the end result (i.e., the ends justifying the means). We have to first build our moral character to protect against our decision making becoming immoral even though the result might benefit others.

Counting not just the risks and benefits to others but also the personal risks of unwelcome outcomes, both short term and long term, will help us reach for the ultimate win-win decision and help us make compromises between risk and reward.

2. See Exodus 20:1–17.
3. See Matthew 5–7.

Follow Through Rightly

Going through a thoughtful and moral decision-making process is not enough; we must also execute our decision in keeping with our character and moral code. Making a decision to fund a retirement account is a wise and moral decision, but cheating on your taxes or buying stock on insider information is not a moral way of achieving your moral goal. You must manage your resources wisely and rightly.

Developing the different aspects of your character and learning to use these five steps effectively in decision making is like becoming an accomplished artist or craftsman. Unfortunately, some people use the words of God like a blunt instrument, wielding them like a sledgehammer for every decision. But in actuality, the Bible is much like a well-stocked tool chest, and each situation and decision potentially requires a different tool from the chest. At various times wood needs to be shaved, sawed, burnt, sanded, stained, painted, or split. You need a different tool and developed skill at wielding it for each unique situation.

The biggest gamble of all in decision-making is allowing fate to make your decisions for you. I don't personally believe in fate, but I do believe in things taking their course amidst inaction.

Some call it waiting on God. They'll go through the decision-making process and then pray for God's blessing, waiting for a sign to proceed, all the while the passage of time closes doors of opportunity on perfectly moral choices that they wanted to pursue. Or did they? Sometimes people's fear of making decisions is so great that they decide to "wait on God," hoping that their inaction will allow God

to work his will and take the pressure off of them to make a decision and live with the consequences. This is a most paralyzing theology that tasks God only with opening doors and robs his ability to close doors. God loves people of character and action!

Given my thousands of hours in casinos, a certain carpenter's life resembles, to me, that of a masterful gambler with the perfect system in dealing with people. Even when Jesus seemed to be losing, he was winning. In his interactions with sinful people, one time he would turn over tables in rage, and another he would simply draw in the sand. We must learn a system that will ultimately please the Master.

Your Turn to Deal

Why do you need character before you develop your
   decision-making system? How do you build character?

Give an example of how the Bible can be used as a tool
   chest. What is a verse that sounds like a sledgehammer
   and another that sounds like a rubber mallet?

Can you think of a time when you went through a good
   decision-making process but didn't "follow through
   rightly"? How about when a public figure did?

DEALING
WITH BAD
PLAYERS

It is always the secure that are humble.

G. K. Chesterton

In poker, you never know how good you are until you play against the best. Your opponent isn't the casino. The players seated next to and across from you are all trying to take your chips. And you're happy to beat them to it. Even in other casino games that seem to pit all the players against the house, your fellow players can actually turn the tide of the table against you if they don't know how to play. In blackjack, for example, if the players around you don't know what to do with a soft 16, they might just help the dealer make his hand and sink the whole table.

The problem with blackjack is that you can't control who walks up to the table, let alone how they play their hands. On my worst days, I would become impatient with or even belligerent to anyone who dared play their cards in a way that would sink my hand. With a heavy sigh, a roll of the eyes, or even an antisocial, confrontational "Why didn't you hit that?!" I tried to passively or actively "correct" the unwelcome player at the table. But it was always useless, because one truth is inescapable, whether in a casino or in a relationship: you can't truly change other people; you can only change yourself.

In our casino-hectic daily lives, we semi-naturally look to spend time with people who play the game of life like we do and try to avoid others who split their face cards. Surrounding yourself with people who have a proper outlook on life is the first step in winning. Choose your posse wisely, as the kids might say. This is true in tack-

ling a group project at school, in starting or running a business, and in dating and marriage. But we all know from experience that we can't choose our family, our superiors at work, or which server we're assigned at our favorite restaurant. So how can we change the actions and attitudes of those folks to make our lives more enjoyable?

We can't.

Plain and simple, just like in a casino, sometimes you can not only not change who is in your life but you also can't change what they do around you. If someone is mean, inconsiderate, rude, or indifferent, or steals from you, or mocks what you believe in—you name it—you can't control their actions, only how you respond to them. And the world says,

Get even.

Stand up for your rights.

Look out for number one.

Revenge is sweet.

Like a serpent whispering in our ear, society tells us there is no player in the game more important than ourselves. But for those who want to win the game of life by following a system laid out by God himself, we have a different strategy that we too often forget in the casino's parking lot. Eugene Peterson paraphrased some of Jesus's words in the Sermon on the Mount this way:

> You're blessed when you're at the end of your rope. With less of you there is more of God and his rule. You're blessed when you feel you've lost what is most dear to you. Only then can you be embraced by the One most dear to you. You're blessed when you're content with just who you are—no more, no less. That's the moment you

Soft: In blackjack, the ace can have a value of either 1 or 11, whichever helps the player. So when a player is dealt an ace and a 5, this would be called a "soft 16" because no card will bust the player's hand. They would have no reason to stand on a soft 16 since the dealer must draw to make a 17 or better.

find yourselves proud owners of everything that can't be bought. . . . You're blessed when you care. At the moment of being "carefull," you find yourselves cared for. . . . You're blessed when you can show people how to cooperate instead of compete or fight. That's when you discover who you really are, and your place in God's family. You're blessed when your commitment to God provokes persecution. The persecution drives you even deeper into God's kingdom. Not only that—count yourselves blessed every time people put you down or throw you out or speak lies about you to discredit me. What it means is that the truth is too close for comfort and they are uncomfortable. You can be glad when that happens—give a cheer, even!—for though they don't like it, I do! And all heaven applauds.[1]

These are the house rules. When dealing with people who play the game of life poorly through ignorance, you have an opportunity to come alongside them and teach them the game in love. What if

1. Matthew 5:3–5, 7, 9–12 Message.

no one ever came to your aid when you were still a newbie? And in dealing with those who enjoy contention or simply enjoy ruining the game for others, God's Word says you are to expect such attitudes and count yourself blessed, for you are playing the game rightly. It is the truth in your life that draws them to you and at the same time makes them uncomfortable around you. You can never change someone else; leave that to God and the other person. If you really want to wear that WWJD bracelet, let's take a read to what Mr. Concrete Sandals himself (Peter) had to say about what Jesus actually *did* when confronted with "bad players":

> To this you were called, because Christ suffered for you, leaving you an example, that you should follow in his steps. "He committed no sin, and no deceit was found in his mouth." When they hurled their insults at him, he did not retaliate; when he suffered, he made no threats. Instead, he entrusted himself to him who judges justly.[2]

Think about it this way: people can insult you, be careless with your feelings, and show reckless disregard for your interests all day long, and all the arguing in the world won't change them. And why should you care if it does? Are you trying to please men, or God?[3] **If you are trying to please men, remember, there are an awful lot of them with varying definitions of what's right and what they want. Your goal is to honor your Father, to care more about him and what he says about you than about what they say, and to *love your enemies in return*.** Jesus says it himself:

2. 1 Peter 2:21–23 NIV.
3. See Galatians 1:10.

> But I tell you who hear me: Love your enemies, do good to those who hate you, bless those who curse you, pray for those who mistreat you. If someone strikes you on one cheek, turn to him the other also. If someone takes your cloak, do not stop him from taking your tunic. Give to everyone who asks you, and if anyone takes what belongs to you, do not demand it back. Do to others as you would have them do to you.[4]

Why do I have to love the rotten players in life, especially the ones who make my life miserable on purpose? Why can't we just choose our friends and family wisely and avoid or tell off every person who comes into our life and doesn't meet our standards? Jesus goes on to say,

> If you [just] love those who love you, what credit is that to you? Even "sinners" love those who love them. And if you do good to those who are good to you, what credit is that to you? Even "sinners" do that. And if you lend to those from whom you expect repayment, what credit is that to you? Even "sinners" lend to "sinners," expecting to be repaid in full. But love your enemies, do good to them, and lend to them without expecting to get anything back. Then your reward will be great, and you will be sons of the Most High, because he is kind to the ungrateful and wicked. Be merciful, just as your Father is merciful.[5]

If Jesus is truly your model, you also should know that he was also capable of rebuke and righteous anger, like when he turned over the tables in the temple. But these controlled outbursts were rare,

4. Luke 6:27–31 NIV.
5. Luke 6:32–36 NIV.

Indeed, what could be more ludicrous in
a vast and glorious universe like this than
a human being, on the speck called earth,
standing in front of a mirror trying to find
significance in his own self-image?

John Piper

strategic, and nothing personal—only situations when he himself wasn't offended but the offense was against his Father and his Father's house. Take his turning over the tables of the moneychangers in the Temple, for example. The offense wasn't against Jesus but against his Father's house.[6]

There is nothing you can do to completely avoid life's bad players, let alone change them. But you can respond to those players in love, because God first loved us even when *we* were unlovable. And if you let others' words and actions offend you or you seek to protect your "self-worth," that's really just folly since our worth should be in God, not in how others view us or how we view ourselves.

6. John 2:13–16

96

Your Turn to Deal

Why shouldn't we "fix" anyone we encounter who needs fixing?

Why doesn't God want everyone to like us?

What do you say to the person who says this is a wimpy approach to dealing with mean people?

**Failure is only the opportunity
to begin again more intelligently.**

Henry Ford

et black, win black." Substitute the color/denomination of choice here (black = $100), and this is a common tidbit of questionable wisdom with a commonsense application: you win what you wager. In less monetary proportions, if you want big results, you've got to wager big effort. There is no such thing as a get-rich-quick-with-little-effort system in gambling or in life.

Ask yourself this question: do I give one hundred percent effort every day in everything I do? When I ask myself this question, I have to give an honest answer of "Not even close." Why not? Well, because what if my effort is wasted? Why should I give my maximum effort when others around me aren't? What if there's no payoff for *me*?

Simply put, effort involves risk. And as we've seen before, when something involves risk, that means there is an inherent danger or potentially unwelcome outcome in store for us. When you give one hundred percent of yourself at work, in a relationship, or in pursuit of a tangible goal *and you fail*, it means you didn't measure up. If you procrastinate, party too much, or put other less-important activities before your goals, you have a built-in excuse if you fail. Whenever I see professional athletes implode on or off the court, the first thing I think is, "That guy is afraid of failure." He's afraid to say no to his old life, posse, and success-impeding habits. Afraid to turn in early when his team is on the road. Afraid to put his all into watching game film, doing off-season workouts (sans pharmacy), and keep-

> **Atychiphobia:** a persistent, abnormal, and unwarranted fear of failure, despite the understanding by the phobic individual and reassurance by others that there is no danger in attempting the task

ing a team-first attitude. Because if he does all that and fails to win championships or deliver when the game is on the line, he has no one to blame but himself.

On the other hand, have you ever noticed how an athlete's stats and effort trend upward when they are in a "contract year"? You know, when it's the last year of their contract and they're in the middle of contract negotiations or about to become a free agent? Ever done the same thing? Maybe not for a gajillion dollars, but how about the week before performance reviews or when a promotion becomes available? Sure, you've always done a good job, but now you're busting your hump for the promotion that's suddenly become available. Why? Because your "extra" effort to land the promotion is suddenly worth the risk and the potential payout.

This phenomenon simply illustrates that we've calculated that the reward outweighs the risk of not performing to our potential. The sad thing is that outside of our "contract year," most of us just don't think it's worth it to prepare or perform to our potential. We consistently fold our hands until a contract year, then we move all in with our effort. I have to admit that I've always struggled in this area, from asking, "When will I ever use calculus?" when I was in high school to turning it on when I could smell a goal and then kicking back and coasting once I got (or didn't get) the job.

Yet as an employer, manager, and even consumer, somehow I expect to get maximum effort from the people I've contracted to do work for me. From the waitress at the BBQ joint to my literary agent (I love you, Chris), I have a huge blind spot when it comes to my expectations of people working for me versus when I'm working for others. I'm working on it, but it's also a major reason why I'm now self-employed!

Now don't get me wrong, my favorite sports are team sports. Volleyball, football, and baseball are all dear to my heart (and big screen TV) not to mention that our company Hungry Planet wouldn't have grown exponentially without excellent partnerships and teamwork with publishers, agents, and retailers. I love collaboration and groups succeeding together rather than one individual hero winning all by his lonesome. For me, putting out maximum effort could've happened when I was working for others, but I didn't fully learn the lesson until I stopped drawing a steady paycheck.

What's worse than fearing the risk of effort? How 'bout instead of calling it the risk of effort, we call it the risk of **trying**. Isn't that even more pitiful? Makes you picture an adult attempting to convince a little kid to just **try** a bite of vegetables.

I hate brussels sprouts, but my wife absolutely loves them. The smell of them steaming in the kitchen makes me want to retch. True confession time: I've actually never even **tried** brussels sprouts. The smell is enough to convince me that the risk of putting them in my mouth is not going to outweigh the outside chance of culinary bliss. So once again, there we have it: danger vs. payoff. Not much

payoff for me in brussels sprouts except the health benefits. And really, can't that be made up for in other foods, say in nutritionally enhanced doughnuts or pizza?

The key to mastering the risks involving effort is mastering the fear of failure. The payoff for achieving the goals at the end of your efforts is obvious. But being able to accept that you just might not be right for your latest crush, that job opening, or the MVP award just means that a better hottie, occupation, or major kudos may be waiting right around the bend. Sometimes a simple approach to setting goals will help chip away at the fear of failure and allow you more freedom to take risks.

◇◇◇◇◇◇◇ USING YOUR CURRENT JOB AS A BUY-IN ◇◇◇◇◇◇◇

The career you've got right now gives you one big thing, whether you hate your job or not: stability. That's a word that just screams risk, doesn't it? So let's all resolve to quit our jobs to fully pursue our passion, right? Wrong. But how about risking our free time to pursue what we ultimately want to do with our work? Use your current job's stability as a "buy in" to the career you really want. Risk giving up sitting in front of the TV a few hours a day and give up some nights and weekends to start giving your dream job a chance to take root. When you start missing opportunities to make cash doing the thing you love because you've still got your old job, guess what? It's time to quit and time to love your job.

Your Turn to Deal

Use this exercise to demystify and de-horrify your goal:

Describe what you want to accomplish, with as many specifics as possible.

Describe your goal in clear terms that can be measured.

Detail how much effort, energy, and discipline you will commit to accomplishing the goal.

Describe how and why your goal is obtainable.

Record when you will complete the goal and how often
you'll review your progress, and break longer-term
goals into smaller chunks with their own dates of
completion.

Note: the ultimate goal in any person's life should be loving God,
and we won't fully succeed at that until we see him face-to-face,
but setting goals not only will help you accomplish more but also
establishes discipline and security in our lives.

Wisdom is nothing more than healed pain.

Robert Gary Lee

Whether it's watching the guy on third base splitting sixes or seeing your opponent in poker call your bluff, nothing is more paralyzing than knowing that pain is coming. Whether it's a girlfriend who says, "We need to talk," a boss who calls you to his office and says, "Shut the door behind you," or a nurse heading toward you with a syringe, our face goes white, our gut hurts, and our hopes fade when we anticipate the worst.

As my wife, Hayley, can attest, people have different definitions and tolerance levels for physical pain. When we first got married, she was a pretty big wimp when it came to pain. Her whole life revolved around avoiding discomfort. When we traveled, she would need her neck pillow, a specific head pillow (not hotel issue), and a thin pillow that she slipped between her knees when she was on her side. Her knees "hurt" if she didn't have that pillow. And let's not forget her blindfold. I remember one trip where she forgot her blindfold so I had to put a towel over the microwave clock so it wouldn't brighten the room at night.

Um, yeah.

Now before you think I'm picking on Hayley too much, I have to tell you that this is coming from a guy who would self-destruct his relationships so he wouldn't have to go through the "pain" of breaking up with women!

Pillow Girl 1, Self-Destructo 0.

Third base: The betting position in blackjack on the left-most side of the table. This player plays his hand last, right before the dealer reveals his hand. If the dealer must draw a card, third base can potentially control which card the dealer will draw by the way they play their hand—i.e., hitting or not hitting.

I mentioned the pillow story so we could fast forward two years to see a woman who went through thirty-five hours of labor with no pain meds, plus another five hours with an epidural that wore off after three hours, and then she ended up getting a C-section. All this for a girl who had never broken a bone in her body or stayed a night in a hospital. Sure, she still has most of her nocturnal accoutrements, but she also has been known to fall asleep sitting up in bed with our daughter on her lap and to catch extra z's in the back seat of our SUV in the middle of running errands just because our daughter is finally asleep in her car seat.

So how is it that I married the girl from "The Princess and the Pea" and now she sleeps like Homer Simpson, jaw open and all? She simply found that for her, the fear of physical pain or discomfort is outweighed by the emotional pain associated with potentially not meeting our daughter's needs. And I must state for the record that she is one of the most selfless people I've ever met and an amazing wife and mother! (For more on the physical, see "No Pain, No Game" on page 153.)

So is the fear of pain merely a survival instinct we can't override without a greater issue of survival (like protecting the health of a child)? Perhaps, but I think once again that the issue lies in what our definition of pain is. When I moved from casual gambler to problem gambler and finally became a pathological gambler, my steady slide was accelerated by my need to avoid or numb pain. For most logical, healthy people, the massive debt, absent work ethic, and criminal behavior I was accumulating as a result of my casino adventures would more than qualify as pain. But for me, the pain lay elsewhere, and my addiction hid the hurt, much like Novocain masks a toothache but doesn't pull the tooth. (Also see "Addicted to Risk," page 121.)

When looking at how you handle emotional risk, it's important to look at what you most fear and what causes you the most pain. Then, instead of avoiding those areas, consider if those areas of pain and fear are worth managing or even conquering. I have no doubt in my mind that unless it also motivates you to be better, any fear that paralyzes you is a sin.

For me, my biggest emotional fear has always been that people will not like me. On the one hand, the fear allowed me to develop a pretty good sense of humor and the ability to make entertaining conversation in any situation. But the dark side of this fear was that I rarely said no. I took on too much responsibility at work. Even if I didn't see a relationship working out, I still wouldn't break things off. I would give people the answer they wanted to hear instead of my true opinion.

The simple way to overcome a fear is to do the exact opposite—in my case, start saying no and start expressing what I really think instead of what others want to hear. At times I'm sure I've overcorrected, and others have seen me as opinionated or just a royal pain, but they don't know the life I lived before I embraced a passion for living out a true version of my life. Still, I have to be careful about going overboard with truth telling. For example, consider the phenomenon of "keeping it real." That's the reality TV catchphrase of the day for saying whatever you want with little or no regard for people's feelings or the context of the situation. This perversion of truth telling is self-centered and aggressive and has little if any compassion for others.

◇◇◇◇◇◇ **"PHYSICAL" FEARS VS. EMOTIONAL FEARS** ◇◇◇◇◇◇

Heights	Failure
Spiders	Acceptance
Flying	Commitment
Death	Death

Here's another example of fear fighting for you (forgive me in advance for the following potty talk): I once walked into the men's restroom at work and used one of the four vacant urinals to do my business. I heard the door to the bathroom open behind me, and out of the corner of my eye I saw a co-worker buddy walk by and enter one of the stalls. Restrooms being the echo chambers that they are, I heard him accomplish the same task I did, and he emerged to join me at the sinks for synchronized hand hygiene.

"What's wrong with you?" I said (this was obviously *after* solving my problem of speaking my mind). "There were three perfectly good urinals next to me, and you went off hiding in a stall." Completely dizzied by my questioning, he simply responded, "I feel uncomfortable going to the bathroom in front of others. I know it's stupid, but I get 'stage fright.'" After laughing heartily (I know, I'm such a good friend), I proceeded to tell him the story of how my mother did all the potty training in our house since my dad was always gone working two jobs, and it just so happened that she never taught me how to stand and relieve myself.

Now guess who was laughing?!

I continued with the story of how during my first week of school in the first grade, I walked into the boys' bathroom and decided to sidle up to the wall and give this standing up thing a try. In the middle of my activity, some other boys walked in and started laughing hysterically. Unbeknownst to me at the time, you're not supposed to drop trou all the way to your ankles, leaving your six-year-old rump, hamstrings, and calves for all to see!

My friend was now laughing so hard he was crying.

I then told him that after that experience, my first response when faced with that potential embarrassment (no pun intended) was to hide in the stall, literally and figuratively. All because of the fear of what others might think.

Right then and there we made a pact that only confident (and somewhat twisted) men can make: we started to make bathroom runs together. Yes, we were urinal buddies. The point is, he had to demystify and redefine the danger associated with going to the men's room, just like I had done in my not-so-distant past. He had to replace "What if I stand there and someone comes and goes and I'm still standing there with no progress?" with "Will my confidence ever grow if I don't step up and refuse to give in to this silly fear?"

By facing any fear, you begin to use it as a tool to help you become fearless. Then instead of fear driving you into a stall to hide, it becomes a positive motivation to change and live life in the light of day. Whether the fear is big or small, choosing to face it can even melt away the paralysis rooted in a childhood experience like mine.

⬦⬦⬦⬦⬦⬦⬦⬦⬦⬦⬦⬦⬦⬦⬦⬦⬦⬦⬦ **CRAPS** ⬦⬦⬦⬦⬦⬦⬦⬦⬦⬦⬦⬦⬦⬦⬦⬦⬦⬦⬦⬦⬦⬦

Rolling dice in the game of craps is a flurry of action, obscure terminology, and dizzying math. Technically the best odds of any table game for the player, an intricate knowledge of the game, the discipline to make small bets with hedge bets (bets against your bets), and an extreme amount of patience make for a good (not lucky) craps player. The problem lies in the often frenetic pace and emotional roller coaster ride (not to mention greed) that engulfs the entire table during a "monster roll." Because of the mind-boggling number of bets a player can make on every roll of the dice, the player's "statistical advantage" over other table games can be lost as quick as you can say "seven."

Let me assert my firm belief that the only thing we have to fear is fear itself—nameless, unreasoning, unjustified terror which paralyzes needed efforts to convert retreat into advance.

Franklin D. Roosevelt

ALL IN

Your Turn to Deal

Try this exercise in emotional adventure:

List one thing that is emotionally risky that you would like to do but have been fearful to try. Speaking in public? Leading a study group? Asking someone out to lunch?

Now list your biggest fear associated with the activity. Are you only concentrating on the "worst-case scenario"?

Would most reasonable human beings with your same moral code be fearful as well? Why or why not? Should that stop you?

Are you giving accurate and equal weight to the pluses
and minuses of the activity, based on having fully
researched the activity?

How would you feel if you successfully pulled off this
emotionally adventurous activity?

Note: if the activity is moral and doesn't hurt others and you've
found your fear has diminished even somewhat, you need to prayer-
fully seek out someone you trust to go on your adventure with you!
Remember, pain is only temporary, and how your brain interprets
pain can be reprogrammed. Living a life of worthwhile risk means
that when you see pain coming, lean into it. If silver or gold could
feel pain, the refining fire of a metalsmith would be excruciating.
But to be refined is to be made more pure and valuable. That's how
we should allow God to use pain when it is unavoidable.

**Success is how high you bounce
when you hit the bottom.**

General George S. Patton

opefully, most of you who pick up this book did so because you're intrigued by risk or fearful of taking risks but don't have a full-blown addiction. As has been evident throughout this book, my risky external behavior simply masked an underlying fear of taking everyday risks. Gambling was my numbing agent of choice—though after a while, it seemed I had no other choice. It had become my addiction.

While *All In* isn't a treatise on the evils of gambling or any other device used for escaping real-world responsibilities, I felt compelled to write a short chapter on recognizing addiction in your life. Much of this is pulled from numerous twelve-step programs or church-based recovery groups. Even if you're positive you don't have an addictive habit in your life, read on; you may have a family member or co-worker who might need your help soon enough.

Here are twenty questions to ask when examining whether a behavior is addictive:

1. Do you lose time from work due to the activity?

2. Is it making your home life unhappy?

3. Do you do it because you are shy with other people?

4. Is it affecting your reputation?

5. Have you ever felt remorse after doing it?

6. Have you gotten into financial difficulties as a result of it?

7. Do you turn to lower companions and an inferior environment when doing it?

8. Does it make you careless of your family's welfare?

9. Has your ambition decreased since doing it?

10. Do you crave it to escape?

11. Do you crave it for comfort?

12. Does it cause you to have difficulty in sleeping?

13. Has your efficiency decreased since doing it?

14. Is it jeopardizing your job or business?

15. Have you ever had a complete loss of memory as a result of it?

16. Has your physician ever treated you for it?

17. Do you do it to build up your self-confidence?

18. Do arguments, disappointments, or frustrations create within you an urge to do it?

19. Have you ever had an urge to celebrate any good fortune by doing it?

20. Have you ever considered self-destruction or suicide as a result of doing it?

If you or someone you know answered yes to at least seven of the twenty questions, that's called addiction.

While various twelve-step programs offer a similar road to recovery, I quite like the following eight Christian principles centered on the Beatitudes. More information can be found at www .celebraterecovery.com.

1—Realize I'm not God; I admit that I am powerless to control my tendency to do the wrong thing and my life is unmanageable.

"Happy are those who know they are spiritually poor"

2—Earnestly believe that God exists, that I matter to him, and that he has the power to help me recover.

"Happy are those who mourn, for they shall be comforted"

3—Consciously choose to commit all my life and will to Christ's care and control.

"Happy are the meek"

4—Openly examine and confess my faults to God, to myself, and to someone I trust.

"Happy are the pure in heart"

5—Voluntarily submit to every change God wants to make in my life and humbly ask him to remove my character defects.

"Happy are those whose greatest desire is to do what God requires"

6—Evaluate all my relationships; offer forgiveness to those who have hurt me, and make amends for harm I've done to others except when to do so would harm them or others.

"Happy are the merciful" "Happy are the peacemakers"

7—Reserve a daily time with God for self-examination, Bible readings and prayer in order to know God and his will for my life and to gain the power to follow his will.

8—Yield myself to God to be used to bring this Good News to others, both by my example and by my words.

"Happy are those who are persecuted because they do what God requires"[1]

1. Quoted from http://www.celebraterecovery.com/8principles.asp.

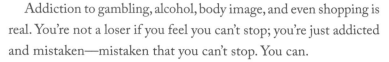

Addiction to gambling, alcohol, body image, and even shopping is real. You're not a loser if you feel you can't stop; you're just addicted and mistaken—mistaken that you can't stop. You can.

Admitting that you need help and seeking out help is your first step. It's important to go to someone who is intimately familiar with your specific addiction, because addicts are expert liars, and addicts of the same substance tell the exact same lies and use identical logic. Having someone who can call you out and see through your sin and sickness will save you time and money and speed you on the road to recovery when you're ready.

And don't dismiss God's power in all of this. All "anonymous" self-help groups embrace that they, along with their efforts, need help from "the God of your own understanding" and recite at least the first part of the Serenity Prayer at every meeting:

> God grant me the serenity
> to accept the things I cannot change;
> courage to change the things I can;
> and wisdom to know the difference.

Not as widely known, here is the continuation of the prayer:

> Living one day at a time;
> enjoying one moment at a time;
> accepting hardships as the pathway to peace;
> taking, as He did, this sinful world
> as it is, not as I would have it:
> Trusting that He will make all things right
> if I surrender to His Will;
> that I may be reasonably happy in this life

and supremely happy with Him
forever in the next.
Amen.

Whether you have bad form in your golf swing, in managing your finances, or in managing your mental or spiritual health, it's monumentally important to recognize you have a problem and then to find a qualified professional to help you correct a problem. With the exception of your back swing, most wrong behavior in your life has a spiritual element attached. Seek out someone who both understands your addiction and wants to find the underlying spiritual problem.

There are no stains on the pages of tomorrow.

Grady B. Wilson

Your Turn to Deal

Have you ever known someone with an addiction? How did it change your relationship?

If you had to guess, to what addictive habit do you think you're most vulnerable? Why?

If someone came to you for help with an addiction, what would you do?

Marriage is an alliance entered into by a man
who can't sleep with the window shut
and a woman who can't sleep with the window open.

George Bernard Shaw

There's one thing to do in a casino besides gambling or eating: you're guaranteed good people-watching. You see all kinds from all walks of life chasing or running from a variety of things, or so it seems. You can see an old lady jump up and down drawing blackjack on a $5 hand; she gets paid $7.50. Right next to her is a man who stoically gets the same 3:2 payout, this time on a $500 bet. He almost looks depressed.

That's the very odd thing about gambling—the more often you gamble, the more antisocial you become. You start going to have a good time with friends, but for many the trip becomes more and more about losing yourself in the game. The novelty wears off, the neon burns out, and you're left with the sobering fact that most people lose. That's because gambling is simple math wrapped and marketed in illusion. Casinos will even tell you that gambling is *entertainment*. In other words, "Enjoy yourself while we take your money!"

Consider the tales of two gamblers. One is a man who comes to town and stays at the casino for a convention. He wanders through the slots and table games and is enraptured and dizzied by the sights and sensations all around him. Trying his hand at blackjack, even the first bad shoe is washed over by a fresh shuffle where hope springs eternal.

Meanwhile, a grizzled veteran of the game, maybe even a local, may be sitting next to Mr. Wayne New-to-town getting dealt the

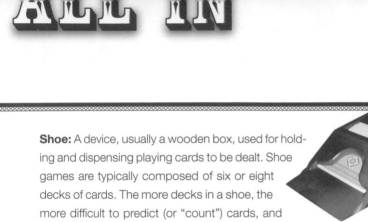

Shoe: A device, usually a wooden box, used for holding and dispensing playing cards to be dealt. Shoe games are typically composed of six or eight decks of cards. The more decks in a shoe, the more difficult to predict (or "count") cards, and the more hands can be dealt between shuffles.

same cards but too wrapped up in his past losses to appreciate the moment. His mind is not trained on the fact that his stack just got bigger, because the numbers don't lie, and he knows losing hands are coming.

In an eerie sort of way, love is a lot like gambling. Except for the lotto winners of love, the great majority of us have lived the two lives of our two men of chance. Certainly Mr. New-to-town's experience rings a bell, and to some degree maybe Gary Grizzled's. A few of us might even have felt addicted at times. See if one of the following statements has ever applied to you:

> You tried to convince someone you were right for them even after they described all the things wrong with you.
>
> You compromised your moral convictions to pursue or stay in a relationship.
>
> You started to look for someone else to date before your current relationship was over.
>
> You have ever said, "I can't be alone."

You stopped spending time with longtime friends and
    only spent time with your love interest.

You used manipulation or deceit in attempts to keep a
    relationship.

You constantly issued ultimatums to have the other
    person demonstrate their devotion.

If you said yes to any of these, it's likely that you've put yourself
at risk for a love addiction at some point in your life. This list was
easy for me to make since most of these have applied to me at some
point. So why are we so susceptible to loving the wrong way? What
is the undeniable pull of love?

True love is the fuel of heroes.

True love accepts us without regard to flaws or shortcomings.

We all want to be heroic.

We all are afraid of not being accepted for who we are.

As the youngest of six kids, I was a "miracle baby" or "love child"
(take your pick), conceived to parents who were in their late forties at
the time, probably with a Frank Sinatra album in the background. So
my dad was sixty-four when I graduated from high school. Growing
up, I had a dad who couldn't really play sports and all with an active
son. So I vowed, "I'm going to get married younger and have kids
sooner so they can have an active dad." I wanted not only to "fix" the
problems of my childhood by doing this but also to make my mark
on history and my family tree by assuring my relevance.

Not mature enough for marriage and despite serious doubts, I
plunged into holy matrimony at age twenty-three with my timeline
running the show instead of wisdom, morals, or common sense.

Trying to rectify the "sins" of my father and not having a clear understanding of the definition of love proved fatal to my marriage.

I proved fatal to my marriage.

After my divorce, I basically gave up on "traditional" love, tossing my moral compass into my Dead Sea of Relationships. This time I took the "bad boy" fast track to love, shacking up with one girl after another. One thing that goes through the mind of many a single is a love timetable that is written and modified to provide the key to happiness and love in life. The timeline starts in your youth, with a target age for marriage, kids, career, and retirement. But usually God makes you throw that timeline out until you conquer your fears and show that you understand what love really is and that it's the greatest tool he uses to make you a better person and help you know him.

So many take the same reckless risks of love that I took, hoping that love will make them happy. And love can make you happy if you let God love you and you start to love others the way God intended.

Maybe we should take a look at arguably the most popular definition of love, read at weddings around the world.

Love Defined:

> Love is patient and kind. Love is not jealous or boastful or proud or rude. Love does not demand its own way. Love is not irritable, and it keeps no record of when it has been wronged. It is never glad about injustice but rejoices whenever the truth wins out. Love never gives up, never loses faith, is always hopeful, and endures through every circumstance.[1]

1. 1 Corinthians 13:4–7.

Here's our two-part exercise if we're *serious* about love. Part one is singling out what love is and isn't. Love is (or isn't) the following:

Love is	Love isn't
Patient	Jealous
Kind	Boastful
Rejoicing in truth	Proud
Never giving up	Rude
Never losing faith	Demanding
Hopeful	Irritable

And lest we forget, Jesus himself said the greatest commands from God were to love God and love others as ourselves. Now here's the second part of our exercise: realizing that God *commands* us to love. I totally missed this in my youth (which, like for too many men today, extended into my thirties). I thought, "How can I love this person when they stabbed me in the back? I just don't feel like it."

But God can't command feelings, only my actions. If I commanded you right now to be giddy, you'd probably stare back at the book with a blank face saying, "Dude, you said 'giddy.'" Since God commands us to love, love must be an action that we're capable of performing regardless of how we feel personally and even how we feel about the other person.

You see, Jesus even said, "Love your enemies. Do good to those who hate you. . . . Do you think you deserve credit merely for loving those who love you? Even the sinners do that!"[2] **If a command to love our enemies doesn't reinforce that love isn't simply an emo-**

2. Luke 6:27, 32.

tion, I'm not sure what will! Since I believe in semi-full disclosure, here is a list of my enemies who I am supposed to love:

- the guy who won't move out of the fast lane
- the woman who won't use her turn signal
- the repairman who shows up outside his 1:00–4:00 p.m. window
- my wife returning from the mall with something she "saved $100 on"
- our dog Moose after he digs a hole
- the guy who invented the Diaper Genie that leaves me struggling to tie that stupid knot

It's the strangest thing, but being married sometimes feels like sleeping with the enemy. But saying "I just don't love her anymore" in the midst of marital problems isn't identifying your feelings; it's identifying your disobedience. You're treating love as an emotion instead of an action, and we all know what can happen when emotions rule instead of God!

I did this. I was guilty of giving up on my first marriage. When Hayley and I started dating, I told her, "The biggest mistake in my life was getting a divorce." Now, this wasn't me pining for my ex. She and I had long since moved on, ten years prior. And instead of Hayley interpreting my statement that way and being uncomfortable or turned off, this was a freeing statement to her ears. She translated that statement (as it was intended) as "I didn't have the same definition of marriage then as I do now." I didn't know that love is an action that is necessary even when you don't feel like it, and if I had known, I'd have made my actions match my vows.

Feeling free to make such a statement (and own it) to Hayley demonstrated that I had all but conquered the two stooge-like fears that had moved my love life from a twisted slapstick of eye-gouging blindness to a healthy perspective on love: insecurity and rejection.

Insecurity

Whether related to your looks, career, smarts, or skills in conversation with the opposite sex, doubts about your potential worth or value to another person can keep you from pursuing love. Your insecurities can also make love and life miserable for the other person once you're in a relationship. A constant need for affirmation gets old, and a one-question pop quiz for being healthy and ready for love is the following:

Insecurity is attractive: true or false?

We all have faults and shortcomings. Make a list of what is changeable and what is not, and then get to work on your personal growth. Remember that true security doesn't come from a razor-sharp intellect or awesome abs but rather from knowing who created us and who we serve. Seeing God's purpose in our lives and having esteem in him beats glorifying your "self"-esteem any day.

Rejection

This is a biggie for a lot of people and was at the root of most of my messy breakups. Whether you're fearful of receiving rejection or of dishing it out, I've dedicated a whole chapter (and book) to this—see "When Your ATM Dumps You," page 143.

When you look at how God defines love and start living it out, you begin your journey of understanding why love is so spectacular. You start dishing out love like a hero and start feeling that unconditional acceptance from the One who created you. Living and sacrificing for someone else is the road toward seeing God's true character and feeling that love in return—first from God, then from the love on your life on this earth. Love is about risking that God's commands are for good and that he's worth trusting for your security, worth, and companionship.

Your Turn to Deal

When you were young, what did your love and/or life timeline look like? How has it matched up to your life? Is that a good thing or a bad thing?

Think back to the story of an Italian immigrant asking to marry a girl he had not even met. How do you think their definitions of love and marriage differed from the ones currently used in our culture?

Who in your life do you need to show "love action" toward, even when you're not feeling it?

You have a zero percent scoring average
on shots you don't take.

Wayne Gretzky

When I was the most depressed in my life, I turned to gambling, mostly for the escape and to numb the pain I was creating. But imagine if everyone I met at the casino was rude. What if every dealer I lost to laughed at me or a pit boss could be heard saying "Loser!" under her breath as she handed me a meal comp? Quite the opposite happens—casinos strive to give the customer the most welcoming environment on the face of the earth. Drive the strip in Las Vegas and you'll see a customer-oriented theme of one-upmanship. The only rejection a man has to face in a casino is from the credit card company or ATM machine.

Because my wife and I believe that the best use of our mistakes is sharing them so others can avoid making the same ones themselves, we publish a lot of books on relationships and the mistakes we've made. *All In* definitely fits that bill. Since the fear of rejection is such a major player in the Fear Factor game of our lives, here's an introductory taste of one of our books, *The Art of Rejection*, guest starring the beautiful Hayley DiMarco:

> Time and time again, people try to avoid rejection in relationships either by not dating at all or by blurring the lines between friendship and dating. The irony is that rejection is a natural part of life. From our earliest days we remember picking teams in gym class, awkward middle school social events, the stress surrounding a potential prom date, and interviewing for our first job—all involving potential rejec-

tion. Even saying "I love you" to someone for the first time is fraught with rejection peril. Or is it?

Rejection is consistently portrayed as a negative. We hear the rejected say, "It feels like the end of the world" and "I never want to go through this again." We even said things strikingly similar in our not-too-distant pasts. The funny thing is that rejection always makes things better. You heard us: *rejection always makes things better*. If you truly believe that all things work together for good, then you have to believe that even rejection turns out for the good. That's why we see rejection as an art form instead of something that requires healing. Most of the time we hurt from rejection because we didn't have a proper perspective on the situation and we let things get out of control. Guess what? Rejection is your reset button.

"I don't think we should see each other anymore."

Click.

Reboot.

A Rejection Story

by Hayley

Back in college I was going out with this guy for maybe a couple months. I thought everything was just fine. One night we went out on this great date. Fine restaurant, great movie, good conversation. After a wonderful night he took me back to my apartment, walked in, sat down beside me on the couch, and said, "I don't think we should see each other anymore." Gulp! I didn't see that coming. Oh, the agony. I spent the next few weeks trying to get him to understand that I *was* someone that he *should* be dating.

Unfortunately, instead of grasping that the other person was doing us a favor by setting us free to find someone who was truly made for us, we lament over what we've "wasted": time, affection, gifts, and effort, among other things.

We don't know if Thomas Edison was much of a ladies' man, but consider these quotes:

Genius is one percent inspiration and 99 percent perspiration.

Be courageous, whatever setbacks America has encountered, it has always emerged as a stronger and more prosperous nation.

Results? Why, man, I have gotten lots of results! If I find 10,000 ways something won't work, I haven't failed.

Catch that? Edison understood that failure was only not trying. When the first 9,000 or so attempts to invent the lightbulb didn't work, he just considered himself *closer* to his goal. Edison clearly understood the Art of Rejection.

Look, maybe you've recently been dumped or had your ex freak out on you when you tried to break things off, and as a result you're hurting. It was messy, and you don't want to repeat it. We've been there. We're still there! Not from dating (we don't swing) but in business, meeting new people at church, and returning clothes without a receipt, we still deal with rejection almost every day. But that's our point. You can't avoid the *R* word and still lead a full, colorful life.

Yes, this book will offer help to those of you still dealing with hurt. But our hope is that you'll come away from this little read with an authentic love of rejection! Our goal is to make you stop saying things like "I can't believe you're doing this to me!" and "Can't we give it just one more try?" and instead start saying confidently, "Well, I guess you weren't the one" and "Glad I found out now before we got married!"

Before we get started, let's do a little review. Life 101. There are only two outcomes for any relationship with a person of the opposite sex:

1. Marriage
2. Rejection

That's it! Since we only want you to get married once and there are going to be a lot of Mr. and Ms. Wrongs out there, let's learn the art of letting them down the right way and, as the case may sometimes be, accepting rejection ourselves. So sit back and learn from two people who have done it all wrong so you can do it right! Let's begin to appreciate the Art of Rejection.

Now that we've completed our topically related infomercial for our single friends, on a narrower scale (focused on singles), *The Art of Rejection* teaches and encourages you to realize that rejection, just like risk, is unavoidable on earth. God gets rejected here daily. Hey, it's a tough room.

The ultimate story of bouncing back from rejection is Easter. I mean, come on, the Son of God hung on a cross to die a criminal's death and bear the sins of the world . . . talk about getting a pink slip! No greater rejection than that will ever take place. And like I said regarding the fear of pain, Jesus saw it coming; he even sweat blood just thinking about the burden he was about to bear. But he endured it for a purpose, knowing what lay ahead of him: the most triumphant rebound in the history of the world.

I have to say that when a big portion of your life turns out to be a lie (i.e., my gambling), it's very easy to lose all trust from your friends and co-workers. Especially when jail is involved (but more on that later). You hope that people can compartmentalize and see the "old you," the "sick you," the "stupid you," and the "potential you" all separately so your friendship still holds value in their eyes. Understandably, I lost (at least for a time) virtually all my friends, Christian and not. *Big-time rejection.*

My faith was pretty much dormant leading up to that time, but I found new hope sitting in a jail cell reading the tattered old Bible that was part of the out-of-date jail library. I had decided to start reading from the beginning, since I had decided that this was my new beginning. Deeply engrossed in Genesis, I nearly fell out of my bunk when I heard a guard down below in the commons area yell, "DiMarco! Visitor!"

I had no family in the area. The closest people I had to family were my co-workers (from the job where I "borrowed" money) and ex-girlfriends who hated my guts. So it totally blew me away to see a non-churchgoing softball buddy sitting on the other side of the glass with the stereotypical black phone handset to his ear.

"Hi, Unc. Who'd you whack?"

It was Dan, the same guy who balanced his daughter in his hand, now valiantly trying to balance his memory of me with the green-jumpsuit me. Ever the comedian, I cracked some joke about getting back to my new posse and then told him what had happened. For our good-bye, we even did the palms together on the glass thing, giving a lighthearted lift to both inmate and visitor. Jocularity aside, I will forever be impressed with Dan's compassion in visiting me when no one else did and, more importantly, with how he was willing to cast fear aside. Fear of visiting a county jail. Fear of associating with an accused felon. Fear of being wrong about me.

Rejection seems too tough to bear at times. There will always be people who say you're not good enough for them in a relationship, for a job opening, at a casting call. Maybe you'll even experience rejection from your parents or as a parent. The point is that the fear of rejection can paralyze you from pursuing and achieving success and living life as an open person—open to adventure, open to friendship, open to love, and open to possibilities that God has in store. It's important to note that Jesus endured the greatest rejection of all time. Whether it's finding a mate or inventing sources of artificial light, appreciating the art of rejection instead of fearing it will keep you focused on better things ahead.

Your Turn to Deal

Why do you think some people deal with rejection better than others? Which are you?

What is easier, to be rejected or to do the rejecting? Why?

What have you invented and how long did it take? If you could invent anything, what would it be?

The pain of the mind is worse than the pain of the body.

Publilius Syrus

gambler's currency isn't always money. I've always had, as Maverick said in *Top Gun*, "a need for speed," and if our family ever feels the pull to go to the mission field, I'm sure it will be to Germany so I can slap a Jesus fish on the back of my Audi and witness to the drivers I leave in my dust on the autobahn. But for now, I'll have to settle for the ripe mission fields of the Nashville Metro Traffic School (I'm a two-time alum).

In my younger days, I used to knowingly speed. Especially when I was riding sport bikes, aka crotch rockets. Now *that* was risk. The adrenaline rush of leaning side to side in tight S-turns, the g-forces of opening up the throttle, launching you forward . . .

Excuse me while I collect myself.

You might find this hard to believe, but writing those words actually gave my mind and body a rush!

Growing up, I had parents who *hated* me taking physical risks and often talked or bribed me out of doing so. In elementary school Mr. McMahon, a fifth-grade teacher and the Thurston Bulldogs football coach, came up to me in the hallway and asked if I liked football and if I would go out for the team. I told him I'd like to, but my mom would have a cow (I probably used those exact words) if it was tackle or there was any contact. He said it was only flag football, not tackle, and besides, he'd put me at flanker. At the time I had no idea what a flanker was, but I figured flag football shouldn't be a problem.

Of course, in a classic story of bait and switch, my first day at practice I was put on blocking on the offensive line (evidently a squatty kid as flanker will lose ball games), the only position in peewee flag football with contact. In the third game of the season, I took a forearm to the nose while blocking a defensive lineman twice my size, and there was blood everywhere from my big Italian nose.

That was my last game, of course.

Trying to satisfy my love jones for sports, I begged to go out for Little League under the notion that "football is a contact sport, but baseball is a thinking man's (boy's) game." I promised that I wouldn't get hurt. As it turned out, the coach put me at catcher (squatty kid squats for a living). *Once again, the only position where there can be contact.* But that was fine by me; the few plate collisions I had were exhilarating. I was actually disappointed when guys rounding third would hold up and not slide into home plate.

(Bad rep note: guys on my old city league team from back in the day will attest to my love of collisions and even try to convince you that I leveled an opposing player's twelve-year-old son who was filling in at catcher because they were short a player and would have to forfeit the tournament if they played a player short. He was at least thirteen. And I was safe.)

My mother rarely came to the games for fear of witnessing the moment I became paralyzed from the neck down. Come playoff time, she had to come. And in my first at bat, I took an inside heater to the temple and bled all over home plate.

Who knew I was a bleeder?

A trip to the hospital and twenty-two stitches later, my baseball career was over. That was my first and last season.

Not only is hindsight 20/20, but it's also conveniently susceptible to our personal psychological spin. With that disclaimer out of the way, may I suggest that if we keep others from risking for fear they'll get hurt, they are going to either run from risk the rest of their lives or store up all their energy and drive to risk until they can't contain it anymore. Like me—once I got out of the house, I became a sports junkie, speed freak, and relationship annihilator.

Probably the most surprising thing about my life today is that when I do get a speeding ticket, I'm totally oblivious to the fact that I was speeding. The last time was when I was making a 10:00 p.m. Chinese food and nausea pharmaceuticals run for my pregnant wife.

Speaking from experience with both sides of the coin, I can tell you that people who avoid physical risks for fear of pain are denying themselves reminders that they are alive. We were not created to be robots or to live in a hermetically sealed, pillow-cushioned bubble. When was the last time you actually felt the blood rushing through your veins? Adrenaline was not placed in our bodies just for times of danger!

I know what it's like to use adrenaline to avoid responsibility or to numb the pain in your life. But moderation is the key, not abstinence.

Your Turn to Deal

A healthy physical life lies somewhere between a "No
Fear" and "No Risk" ad campaign. Which direction do
you need to move to create that balance in your life?

What's one physical activity you wish you could do,
but your fear or someone else's is keeping you on
the sidelines? Bungee jumping, skydiving, ballroom
dancing, roller blading, boogie boarding?

If another person's fear is holding you back, write down
why it's important that you exercise your risk muscle
and how you'd share that with the other person.

If the fear is your own, write down who can better
educate you on the ins and outs of the activity. If you
don't know where to start, Google it or call a shop
that specializes in the activity or sells the equipment
needed. Adding to your knowledge about the activity
decreases any fear you might have of the unknown.

Write down a date or deadline to take a lesson and just
do it!

Note: if the activity is moral and doesn't hurt others and you've
found your fear has diminished even somewhat, you need to prayer-
fully seek out someone you trust to go on your adventure with you!
Remember, pain is only temporary, and how your brain interprets
pain can be reprogrammed. Plus, chicks dig scars, and guys respect
a girl who's physically fearless. Just let him continue to get the door
for you, ladies.

A RISK-
FREE LIFE

A ship in port is safe, but that is not what ships are built for.

Benazir Bhutto

Ask any gambler and they'll claim to be a person of faith. Faith in the next roll of the dice, the turn of a card, or their lucky charm. All gamblers exhibit behaviors necessitating faith. Even the occasional prayer to some unknown God of Green Felt can be muttered in the most solemn and desperate of times. The rest of the time, however, a gambler is supremely confident in their own ability to steer their chances to riches.

People professing faith in God is a pretty common thing. Depending on which polls you read, anywhere from 75 to 85 percent of Americans identify themselves as Christians. And if Christians are supposed to follow the teachings of Jesus and his apostles as main tenets of their faith, why is the morality of the U.S. sliding? Is it the other 15 to 25 percent? Hardly. Unfortunately, identifying with an ethical standard and living by it have become two totally different things.

The truth is that most people, Christian or not, are fearful of living a godly life. They are afraid that fun times will be over, afraid they'll never get what they want, afraid they'll have to develop (gulp!) self-control. And they are unable to overcome the fear of bondage and lack of freedom they associate with living by God's standards. These people who are fearful or cynical of leading a godly life have a picture in their minds of their lives being robbed of the excitement and risk that they long for. And you know who's to blame?

Christians, mostly.

Answer the following statement, true or false: living a full and blessed life of faith in God is living a life mostly absent of risk.

How did you answer? If you said "false," then help me cheer on the "true" folks who are correctly taking a risk for higher enlightenment! There are two major ways that Christians misunderstand risk in their lives:

1. I should follow God's will, so if I wait for it, poof! No risk involved.
2. God wants me to be happy and satisfied, so if I'm not getting what I want, either it's not his will or I'm in sin.

The following scenario has happened to my wife and me two or three times over the past year. A Christian couple will come up to us and say, "Can you pray for us? We're seeking God's will about a house we'd like to buy, and we just want to wait on him to see if we should buy it."

Translation: we love God and want to be faithful to his will for our lives.

Alternate translation: we don't think God wants us to take risks, so we're waiting for a "go" sign before we proceed.

In every case, Hayley or I ask the same questions:

"Can you afford it?"

"Do you want it?"

"Will it make your family and spiritual lives better?"

"If you said yes to all three and you've used wisdom and truth to reach those answers (you really *can* afford it), do you have faith that God will close the door on the deal if he doesn't want you to get the house?"

In *every* situation, the couple's eyes brightened because they felt freed to make the decision. One couple lost the house to another buyer but found an even better fit the next week.

God provides example after example of his expectations that we should use the gifts that he has given us to be discerning and that we are to become wise people. When two women came to King Solomon to resolve a custody dispute, he didn't pray for wisdom, consult Scripture, or wait for a sign, because he had already studied Scripture and developed wisdom and knew that God expected him to take risks while using his gifts wisely. Telling the women to cut the child in half so they could equitably share the child was not a biblical command found in First Copperfield chapter 3. It was a perfectly clever (cleaver?) display of the wisdom of man developed *through* God's Word. Of course, the true mother stopped the act, giving the boy to the other woman, allowing Solomon to deduce that the merciful woman was indeed the child's mother.

In a number of stories God allows people to go through trials, even when they don't seem deserved. The story of Job is a familiar one, and in his cries of "Why me?" and "What have I done wrong?" is the subtext of a man who expected that if he followed God's law to the letter, his life would be not only blessed (as it was before he was tested) but also devoid of this kind of "undeserved" risk of faith.

You probably don't have to look far in every church in the world to see someone who is crippled with affliction or a consistent streak of bad luck and to realize that sometimes bad things happen to good people—and due to no fault of their own. Yet so many Christians, unable to explain the phenomenon of Job or simply wanting to sell a bill of goods for a feel-good or prosperity gospel, eventually come out and say, "If you accept God and live by these rules, you'll live risk-free!" or "God wants you to have everything you want now."

I hate to say this, but God says that you'll actually live your best life *later*. Eden is where it was, and heaven's where it's at. Where we are is only temporary and an opportunity to lead, serve, and be sanctified (made ready) for heaven.

In essence, many in the Christian faith are saying, "God created us to be happy." But happy about what? Happy that we get whatever we want, or happy that we have more than we deserve? The biggest risk we face in our lives is risking that our "self" is not who we should be living for but rather we should be living for our God.

What makes him happy?

For what purpose can I serve him?

How can I share him with others?

What is more risky, having faith in yourself or having faith in God? Think about it, because like it or not, when we don't follow God's guidance for our lives, we're basically saying, "Living life his way is too risky. I guide my life better myself." I know all too well how life works when it revolves around Michael having control of the wheel and the GPS navigation system is switched off or not installed. It's not pretty, and people are bound to get lost or even hurt. Been there? Done that? Still there?

True happiness on this planet isn't possible unless you constantly have your destination in mind and are open to "detours" you hadn't anticipated. Heaven should be your destination, and nothing says the road that takes you there is a smooth one, but living in obedience to God's commands provides the most direct route.

Your Turn to Deal

When making a decision, at what point do you pray for
guidance? Is your prayer a prayer for an answer or one
for God's blessing on your decision? Why?

King Solomon has been called the wisest man who's ever
lived. Who is the wisest person you've ever known?
How are they wise? How did they get that way?

What does "living your best life later" mean?

Never let the future disturb you. You will meet it, if you have to, with the same weapons of reason which today arm you against the present.

Marcus Aurelius

Ignorance is bliss. At least to the casinos it is if you, the gambler, are the ignorant one. A secret little known to those other than professional gamblers and gambling regulars is this: if a dealer in the casino asks you if you want to bet on something optional, it's almost always a sucker bet. That is, the odds are in the house's favor, and the dealer is basically trying to sell you the "extended warranty." The casino is banking on your ignorance—that you'll pony up the "insurance" bet merely because they asked if you wanted it.

Of course, the opposite of ignorance is knowledge, and the opposite of bliss is risk or fear—ergo, knowledge can be risky. In other words, for the ignorant and blissful, knowledge is risky because their bliss may end. When we refuse to acquire knowledge about something we're fearful of, we tend to make bad decisions or no decisions at all. Case in point: "The world is flat."

Thank goodness for explorers like Christopher Columbus who sought out knowledge, or we'd *really* have a population crunch right now! With the growth of the Internet and email usage among average citizens, we regularly face hoaxes, urban legends, and relatives of Nigerian royalty offering a piece of their inheritance if you'll just send them a small processing fee, all wanting to prey on our potential unwillingness to risk acquiring knowledge or playing off of our fear of the unknown.

Our fear of the unknown spills over into our faith life as well. Many people don't study the Bible for fear they can't handle or understand the words of God penned by ordinary men. Others are paralyzed by the fear of the unknown simply because they want to know, *they must know* what's happening next or they feel out of control.

Ah, control.

Isn't that always a root issue when it comes down to our self-interest, self-satisfaction, self-esteem, and self-preservation? That is the Holy Grail that all compulsive gamblers reach for as a tiny representation of their lives: in the casino I feel at peace; I make the decisions.

I'm in control.

Let's face it: we all want to drive, and if we don't get to drive, we all want to hold the map. If there's no map, we want to hear when we're stopping next and for how long. Starting with being told which tree to not eat from in the Garden, if the risk of giving up control is our Achilles heel, the fear of the unknown is the pit bull that's latched onto it.

To get over the fear of the unknown, we have to realize these three truths:

1. You get the map when you're done. Contrary to popular belief, you'll never know your life's map until you reach your final destination. God is beyond all comprehension, and so is his plan for us until we see him face-to-face. Start to embrace your present and future like Lewis and Clark tasked with crossing the uncharted West. Your life is unknown territory, waiting to be discovered.

2. You must press on. You are going to face times when the journey into the unknown seems long or is not leading where you thought it would. When you start to find yourself saying to doubt, fatigue, or fear, "I wish I could quit you!" it's time to take a brief rest, reflect on your journey so far, but not move backwards. In your explorer's journal, write down your fears and discouragements, and immediately follow them with why you must press on and why you trust God to get you to your final destination. Close your journal and get some sleep. Then in the morning, press on.

3. Dependence is a good thing. It's not a matter of you liking it or not; it's just the way it is: just like the sparrow, we are all living a life dependent on God. Try to master cloning all you want; you're never going to be him. Dependence means we learn to lean on him for direction, yes, but also for how we ought to conduct ourselves on the journey and how we treat others we encounter along the way.

God has commissioned this adventure of discovery and given you a book of wisdom not only to help on your journey through life but also to fill you with knowledge of your final destination and the character of the one who commissioned you. At times we can feel like we're on our own in the wilderness, but God created us to live a life without fear and full of adventure, embracing the unknown.

It behooves us to know, to the best of our ability, the rules of the game we're playing and the odds of what our choices may bring. Being more knowledgeable about our Creator and reading the journals of the ones who came before us will bring comfort and peace to our souls when we get weary. But isn't it nice to know that others just like us are walking their trails alongside us or in another part of the forest, currently unseen by us, all traveling to the same destination and with the same purpose? We all travel to please the One who is calling us to the undiscovered country.

Your Turn to Deal

What would you do differently tomorrow if fear of the unknown weren't an issue?

What current explorers or ones from the past are you interested in or currently reading to help you on your journey?

Do you journal consistently? Like Lewis and Clark did, journal all you can on your life's adventure. Jot down the wonders and curiosities that you encounter along the way. If you're extra brave, go high tech and make it a blog with a free service like blogger.com.

PLAYING
WITH THE
HOUSE'S
MONEY

There is risk you cannot afford to take
[and] there is risk you cannot afford not to take.

Peter Drucker

asinos are the largest of shiny objects, but much like those Russian nesting dolls, they're just one shiny object inside another and another and another. They're made of money and things that cost money, and it can all be yours for just a small wager or two. One of the most ingenious ways the house protects its money is by giving it away for "free." Take comps and promotions, for instance. I remember a casino I frequented running a promotion with the local soda bottler in which if you hit a certain hand at the different table games, like blackjack, or a certain roll of the dice, you'd win a 12-pack of soda.

I had a pretty hot hand on the craps table that day, rolling hard ways nonstop. In fact, with every hard four, six, eight, and ten I rolled, if I had a $5 bet on the number, I'd win soda. I was betting on and rolling so many hard ways that they started two towers of soda in the pit area to keep my "winnings" out of the way. The problem was that I was so enamored with hitting all the hard ways and growing my stacks of soda that I forgot about my stacks of chips. You see, I was hitting hard ways but losing my other bets, and it slowly bled me dry.

Having won $800 of the house's money, soon I had lost it all, including my $200 buy-in. I did, however, need to make multiple trips out to my car with thirty-two cases of "free" soda.

Nothing in life is free. Except faith.

◇◇◇◇◇◇◇◇◇◇◇◇◇◇◇ **THE COST OF COMPS** ◇◇◇◇◇◇◇◇◇◇◇◇◇◇◇

Casinos know that if a player is winning, the longer they keep him in the casino, the better the odds that he'll lose the money he won and then some. That's why comps (short for complimentary) like free meals, rooms, fight tickets, and other swag are given to players based on how long they play and how much they bet. Essentially the casino is bribing you to stay and keep playing. Sure, you got a free trip through the buffet, but was it worth losing an extra $500? Sometimes the decisions we make for the temporary and immediate cost us more in the long run. People stay in bad relationships for the comps of companionship, security, or even sex. Comps distract you from assessing your situation rationally. Never, ever take comps.

Probably the riskiest move in life is living without faith. My dad used to tell me that he couldn't understand why people wouldn't believe in God. "Why would you turn down life's great insurance policy? It's free!" he used to say. Great theologian, my dad. It's like the AFLAC duck went to seminary for a week.

But my dad was a commonsense guy and straight shooter who had some experience with real risk (he fought in WWII and served during the Korean War), and I think we all get what he was saying. If you're wrong about God, you just decay into the ground, or your ashes sit in a pot on some mantel. But if you're right, you played with the house's money and won—almost like playing in a free poker tournament where you get to keep your winnings at the end.

NEWS FLASH: life *is* a free poker tournament.

In many of the free no-limit poker tournaments on the Internet, one of the most common grumbling complaints of "real" poker players is that without fail, at least one player will go "all in" on the very first hand of the tournament. And most of the time one to four people call (going all in as well), so after this first hand some lucky guy has half the chips at the table, putting the four or so remaining players at the table at a distinct disadvantage.

While I agree that this takes a lot of the fun and strategy out of the game and reduces the game to a pure coin flip, I also appreciate the ignorant zeal behind the all in first bet. It's not real money! If they win, they've got a commanding lead; if they lose, they just go enter another free tournament and do it all over again. But here's the real deal. While we are truly living this tournament of life on house money, there's one little problem with betting all your chips in a reckless moment.

THE VATICAN BOOK CLUB

I grew up in an Italian/Irish home, so going to Catholic mass was in the blood like wine and whiskey. One time my dad said at the dinner table, "I finished a great book today. I think I'm going to send it to the pope." I remember my mother rolling her eyes and me saying, "You can send him my Atari too. I don't play it anymore, and maybe God will get me an Intellivision." He sent the book (but not my Atari—I had a change of heart), and much to our surprise, my dad got a thank-you letter from the Secretariat of State from the Vatican saying that the pope appreciated the gesture.

This life is the only tournament going. There's no other table to go to if you go all in on the wrong cards for the wrong reasons. So if the reckless risk doesn't kill us, we spend a significant time living in and digging out of the mess we've created for ourselves. I know from experience how easy it is to become distracted from what's important by whispers in our ears or shiny objects. Really, I wonder how dogs even respect us sometimes.

It used to be that man had to play God heads up in life: his holiness versus our good works and obedience, with the prize being a ticket to heaven. And God was a formidable match. Of course, God had an ace up his sleeve in his Son, allowing him to gift us a winning hand, all on the house's money. Have you accepted his gift of "the nuts"—a royal flush, an unbeatable hand that allows you unfettered access to the One who created you?

Heads up: A poker term for when only two players are left, playing head-to-head for all the chips.

Your Turn to Deal

What is a situation you've been in when you've stayed for
the fringe benefits but the core of the situation was
less than desirable?

If you've made God the center of your life, when and
where did that happen?

What does "playing with the house's money" mean to
you?

If you have ever been tempted into evil, fly from it.
It is not falling into the water, but lying in it,
that drowns.

Unknown

For a first-time visitor or a seasoned pro, nothing says action and excitement to the risk-taker like the neon lights of the Vegas strip. Even though I could get more gambling in by taking a morning flight into McCarran, I would purposely fly in late just to glide over the pitch black desertscape and then creep up and pounce on the glow of the city of Lost Wages.

I cannot even imagine trying to describe the lights and sights of Vegas to someone who has never seen it. The majestic fountains in front of the Bellagio, the piercing beam of light emanating from the top of the Luxor pyramid, the gaudy color scheme of the Excalibur, and the "Honey, I shrunk the skyline" sight of New York, New York all provide a visual buffet that rivals the all-you-can-eat culinary fare inside each hotel. At least this was my view at the *start* of my gambling career. But if you think I'm now going to launch into a rant on the evils of gambling, I'm not. You see, the hotels and attractions in Las Vegas *are* marvels to behold. It's just that if you spend enough time around the inner workings of the gaming business (in my case, mangled in the inner cogs of the machine), you know exactly how they pay for their monstrous light bills!

A good gambler's best friend (besides his trust fund or credit line) is the ability to read the signs. The dealer hasn't busted for the last eight hands. The last five times that shooter rolled a hard 4, he crapped out.

Rolling hard ways: Rolling a "hard way" in the game of craps is simply having the two dice land on the same number. "Hard" means that statistically it's more difficult to roll matching numbers than unmatched numbers. To get a roll of 8, for instance, you could roll a 2-6, 6-2, 3-5, or 5-3; those are four different ways to roll an 8 "easy." But rolling a 4-4 is throwing an 8 the hard way. So if both tumble and show a 3, you've got a "hard 6" on your hands. If you're staring at two 2s, that'd be a hard 4, prompting the "stick man" at the table to bark, "Four, the hard way!"

The thing about reading signs and calculating odds in gambling is that they only average out over an infinite amount of time. So when you see a dealer make blackjack (two cards equaling 21) six times in a row, it's statistically improbable it'll happen on hand number seven, *if those are the only hands he's ever dealt.* Chances are this same dealer has dealt millions of hands with only a fraction ending in blackjack for themselves (and the house). Still, those who have lived in casinos can have more than occasional intuitive moments when they can smell that a table is about to go bad and, likewise, when things are about to turn. The problem for gamblers, of course, is all those other non-intuitive moments when you're caught with your chips down.

After the fact, a gambler can always point to the signs that prognosticated their winning streak or demise. Hindsight is, after all, 20/20. But in gambling, no one in the casino forces you to bet. You decide which game to play, which table to play at, how much to bet, when to bet, and when to walk away. Though not-yet-abstinent compulsive gamblers might not realize it, every gambler is in control of when and whether they choose to risk.

In the casino, that is.

There are many parallels between the road of real life and driving through the neon lights on the Vegas strip. At the intersection of Las Vegas Boulevard and Tropicana Avenue is a traffic light controlling the flow and timing of cars and pedestrians. But the intersection of life and risk is much more low tech. There are only signs like "stop," "yield," "merge," and "do not enter." On life's road, every decision is an intersection where we must choose how we will proceed and when. For those sitting at an intersection in life waiting for a sign, there are no "go" signs, only signs of "caution," "danger," or, at best, "proceed at your own risk."

God has already told you what to do. Love him with all you have and love others as yourself. Know him by knowing his Word. Be a good steward of what he has given you, and that includes your wisdom and intellect.

Is it moral?

Does it benefit others in a way you would want to benefit?

When we make wrong turns in life, all is not lost. Because God says that for those who love God and are called to his purpose, he'll work out all things for good.[1] Even though you may have turned left when turning right would've been a more direct route, heavenly satellites are already recalculating and replotting your route, much like GPS navigation. Sure, you might have turned into a rougher part

1. Romans 8:28.

of town or be encountering potholes galore based on your choice, but God can still get you home.

When we are attempting to drive our lives, it's very easy to accept blame for the fender benders of our own making. Much like the strip, the world puts up neon signs to attract, distract, and offer the sexiest of long shots to win at life, all while stroking the ego of self.

You deserve it.

You're unappreciated.

You're missing out.

The same old lies have been whispered in our ears ever since the dawn of man. Jesus was tempted in these exact same ways by the devil himself, as we read in Matthew 4. How did he proceed at this very risky intersection?

After forty straight days of fasting, denying himself nourishment as a sacrifice, Jesus heard the devil say, "If you are the Son of God, change these stones into loaves of bread" (v. 3).

You deserve it.

Then the devil took Jesus to the highest point in Jerusalem and said, "If you are the Son of God, jump off! For the Scriptures say, 'He orders his angels to protect you. And they will hold you with their hands to keep you from striking your foot on a stone'" (v. 5).

Prove you're appreciated.

And lastly, from a peak of a mountain, Satan showed him all of the nations of the world. "'I will give it all to you,' he said, 'if you will only kneel down and worship me'" (v. 9).

You're missing out.

In each test, Jesus was not blinded by the neon lights of temptation. Instead, each time he quoted the very words of God, words of truth that reminded Satan and Jesus himself that:

Feeding our bellies does not sustain us, but God's Word does.

Learning from the mistakes of Adam and Eve, we should not test God.

We should be single-minded, only following him.

Jesus knew that Satan's game was a long shot and following God's Word was a sure thing because he knew and used God's instruction. Temptation and risk don't always go together, but many times they do. Always weigh "Is it moral?" and test it against what God has told you.

When you're calculating the odds and reading the signs, even when you look both ways at that intersection of life and risk, you can still get blindsided. And when we get hurt and it was out of our control, suddenly we're vulnerable. Suddenly we realize we're never completely in control of our lives.

Fear.

Doubt.

Disillusionment.

And it wasn't our fault.

Only miles away from our home in Middle Tennessee, a devastating tornado-spawning storm cut a swath of destruction, leveling homes, businesses, and churches at random. My wife was in that neighborhood just hours before, and we could see the black storm wall move across Sumner County from our home in Wilson County on the opposite side of Old Hickory Lake. Sadly, some of those affected are asking "Why?" not realizing that isn't the operative question in life. Instead, they must face the question "What's next? How can I go on and make a difference?" Thousands of people in our community aren't asking why but are giving their time and resources to do something that is moral and isn't selfish, something that says, "This is what I can do. This is how I can make a difference."

It's helping people make their own "go" signs.

God loves people with passion. God loves people who are good stewards of the gifts that he has given them, and two of those gifts are experience and wisdom. When we wait for God to give us a sign and ignore the tools that we already possess (like his written Word) to make a decision, it insults God and shows how fearful we are of living life in the freedom he has given us. How many more signs do we need?

Your Turn to Deal

List some of the lies you've believed in the past (or are currently struggling with) that correspond to the following:

You deserve it.

You're unappreciated.

You're missing out.

What can you do to keep yourself from believing these lies?

The house doesn't beat the player. It just gives him the opportunity to beat himself.

Nick Dandalos

There's an old saying in the world of gambling: "The house always wins." That's because the odds are always set in the casino, lottery, or race track's favor. Many people think that if the wrong team wins in sports betting, the house can lose its shirt. But in all actuality, the casino sets the odds or "the line" on sporting events so that it will generate equal interest on both team A and team B to balance the action, with many casinos happy just making a percentage or a fee for placing the bet.

Another example is the roulette wheel. You get even money odds for betting on black and the same for betting on red. Seems like a coin flip, a wash for the casino if one guy bets $50 on red and another guy bets $50 on black. One wins $50 on every spin and the other loses $50.

Ahhh, but hold it right there, my young grasshopper. The wise council of elders in the gaming industry have to keep the lights on (and thems a lot of lights!), so they *invented* two numbers to add to the wheel. Zero and double zero. And just by chance they have their very own color, green. These two numbers are the house's edge. Because when they hit, everyone playing red or black loses. The house doesn't always win big, but the more hands that are played and the more bets that are made, the odds and lights of Las Vegas say, the house *always* wins.

Roulette: A game played on a long, narrow table with a spinning wheel on one end. You place your chips on either red, black, odd, even, the first range of numbers (1–18), or the second range (19–36). Sometimes the ranges are even split into thirds. Roulette dealers have no problem accepting bets after the ball is dropped and the wheel is spinning (rolled on the rim in the direction counter to the wheel's direction), but not after they wave their hands and yell, "No more bets!"

When the ball comes to its resting place, the dealer calls the number, places a clear plastic cylinder over the winning number and chips, and then sweeps the board clean of losing bets. Only after this does the dealer pay you.

If the house always wins, how do people win? The funny thing about gambling is that if you're winning, you're either beating the house or beating your fellow gambler. For every jackpot hit, another old lady loses a bucket of quarters. Poker is really one of the only forms of gambling where you stare your opponent in the eye and they're not on the casino payroll. Poker is like gambler cannibalism with the casino stoking the fire and stirring the big black kettle. The house wins merely by collecting the ante or collecting entrance fees for tournaments and only paying out a portion of the fees to the winners.

Living a life of faith is really like playing *for* the house. Is it really possible to play for the house? The only consistent winners I have ever met inside a casino were the people who work there. When I was gambling, I found that many of the dealers were former gamblers who had given it up. They had found that the only way to always win at cards, roulette, or dice was to work for the casino. Every time they clocked out, they were up, even if they'd had a terrible "losing" streak dealing blackjack.

I remember one blackjack dealer who didn't wear his real name on his name tag; instead he had one made that read "Hoover." He got that nickname because players invariably lost all their chips to him as he sucked the chips into the house's stacks. It was uncanny. Likewise, certain dealers always seemed to be in a giving mood when I was at their table. Of course, pit bosses rotate dealers for that very reason.

I know this doesn't make sense statistically, but doesn't it seem to play out in life the same way? Some people just seemed to be blessed all the time, while others are constantly slogging it out, just trying to keep their heads above water. Some cruel and twisted people will tell you that God wants you to prosper. That's more foolish than hitting a hard 19.

God wants us to be good casino employees and stop worrying about how many hands we win and how many we lose and just deal according to his rules. He has the odds stacked in the house's favor, and if we're a part of God's house, we'll end up winning in the end. If we can stop viewing ourselves as players in the casino of life and embrace the vision of working for the owner on the other side of the table, we'll begin to realize that our job is to play the hands according to house rules and not worry about the outcome.

Then, having embraced the only sure thing in the house (working for it), you can begin to bring those seeking long shots and break-the-bank systems to the house's side of the table. With God setting the rules and odds in the game of life, wouldn't you rather play on the side of the house? Because in the end, whoever is left gambling against the house loses.

Your Turn to Deal

Why do you think so many people gamble when the odds are never in their favor?

Lottery jackpot winners have a higher than average rate of divorce, lawsuits over money, bankruptcy, and suicide after winning. Why do you think that is?

What does it mean to "stop worrying about how many hands we win and how many we lose and just deal according to his rules"?

There is a very easy way to return from a casino
with a small fortune: go there with a large one.

Jack Yelton

The funny thing about "borrowing" money from your employer without authorization is that even when you replace it, each time you "borrow" you add a rung on the misdemeanor-to-felony ladder. I was undoubtedly losing my job over the unauthorized draws from work, but if I couldn't get the VCR at the pawnshop back to my workplace before they found out, I would be in possession of stolen goods. I would force their hand and leave them with no choice but to press charges since I was employed by a state university.

Following a couple of weeks of scraping money together after resigning my position, I went to the pawnshop to reclaim the VCR. I could then return it to my old work and tell them a lie—that I had been doing video production at home (which I had done before). When I went in to retrieve the equipment, I handed my ticket to the clerk, and after looking up the tag, he said, "Sorry, but it says here the police department is holding the item as stolen."

My face went white. I immediately called the officer who had interviewed me before and explained what had happened. She said I needed to come in to amend my statement as soon as possible.

Even though I knew the "smart" thing to do was to call a lawyer, I didn't. I confessed to everything. I mean, back when I split those aces and prayed I wanted out! So even though I owed my work no money (except all the lousy work ethic I had given them), I was

**Life, like poker, is a game
of incomplete information.**

charged with felony theft and booked into the county jail, where I would stay until the next day's arraignment.

After donning my new brightly colored clothes and red plastic ID bracelet, I was led with sheet, blanket, and towel in hand to "F-tank," a short-term (one hour to one year) holding tank with two tiers of cells surrounding a common area with picnic tables cemented to the floor. Even though each cell had two steel shelves (that would be the bunks), for some reason I got an empty cell that had just been vacated. As I was getting settled, a young fellow inmate came into my cell and asked why I was so special to not have to share with a "celly." He looked down at my red wristband and said, "Whoa, felony. Never mind, bro." How twisted it seemed that in the midst of a bunch of short-timers with misdemeanors, I got instant respect with that little piece of plastic. That said, God had answered my prayer: he got me out of the casino and completely removed me from any opportunity to gamble, at least for the next twenty-four hours.

That night I had the best night of sleep I'd had in over three years.

My jailhouse conversion wasn't one of simply discovering a personal relationship with God. My conversion was one of embracing that God created us all to be creatures unafraid of risk but mindful of the consequences. That a part of faith is risky because it's believing in things unseen. I realized that life, like poker, is a game of incomplete information. That's why people who represent themselves as having it "all figured out" seldom seem in touch with God and reality.

Like Adam and Eve, I had risked so foolishly that I had seemingly lost it all. This was my Garden of Eden epiphany. And my miniature, corrections-issued bath towel served as my fig leaf. All my life I had been avoiding risking in ways God *wanted* me to risk. Meanwhile, the gravity of avoiding certain decisions kept me by default barreling down a road of reckless risk. But now, instead of awkwardly holding my fig leaf in shame, I decided to carry it in hand to the shower in front of all.

No more hiding in fear.

I was in jail just under twenty-four hours before being ROR (released on my own recognizance). I didn't *have* to shower. But something was pulling me to that upright, stainless steel coffin. I was compelled to become clean. It was my baptism into the world of real risk without fear—not the reckless risk of addiction and avoiding responsibility but the risky business of faith and obedience. That's the moment I began to realize we were all created with a longing to live *All In*.

So six weeks later, and just five years after reaching my big coaching goal, there I was, unemployed, waking up on a futon in the spare room at my friend Sean's house—one of the few friends I still had (and another softball buddy). My new morning ritual wasn't going to the university I loved to coach the sport I loved but rather hopping on the city bus to join a work detail picking up trash on the side of the interstate as part of my plea bargain. For all intents and purposes, gambling had ruined me.

I had ruined me.

Even though I was tens of thousands of dollars in debt and barely able to feed my dog, let alone myself, I was anything but ruined. In fact, I had found a brand new peace and understanding regarding risk. I realized God created us for risk. Our lives are riddled with risk. Risk is unavoidable.

While I was jobless and feverishly looking for employment, I began to write about being lousy in relationships. I figured if you're good at something, you might as well share your expertise with others. And I was great at being bad in relationships. If a relationship was a cello, I played it with the skill of an elephant, leaving pulverized bits of wood in my path. Up until that time, the only thing I had enjoyed writing was rubber checks, but my humor columns started getting read and winning awards on different e-zines on the Internet. I was blogging before blog was a word, and no, it wasn't a moneymaker then either! While I loved my newfound hobby, it didn't put ramen on the table or lamb and rice in the dog dish. But after six months of unemployment, thirty pounds of (involuntary) weight loss, and ten years' worth of spiritual renewal packed into twenty-six weeks, I had a real job: answering customer service calls for $8.50 an hour

All in: Poker term for betting everything you have by pushing all your chips into the pot to win big or lose it all on one hand.

for a Bible software company that had just moved their offices to town. Strangely, I felt on top of the world all over again.

I still dreamed big, but this time I continued working my tail off, I stayed humble, and when I was offered a sweet promotion with tons of travel and (gulp) access to company funds, I had to tell the president of the company my history to keep my recovery going and to face my fears. I'll never forget Bob's words: "We've employed worse."

So within a year of being unemployed and eating on $35 a month, here I was traveling 75,000 miles a year, making more than I ever did at the university, working in publisher relations, and providing training to some of the most influential pastors, seminaries, and speakers in the faith today. And while working on my goals of excelling at work and continuing to grow the hobby that brought me joy (churning out humor columns on relationships), I also worked on turning my Dumbo cello skills into something more Yo-Yo Ma–like (Yo-Yo Mike?). Shortly thereafter, I met a woman holding an executive search for a CEO for her newly established publishing company. The only catch was that she wanted to work side-by-side with her CEO 24/7, meaning marriage was the only option in order to avoid ugly overtime regulations or costly stock options. And it just so happened that Hayley Morgan, founder of Hungry Planet, just happened to be a bestselling coauthor of a funny book on, you guessed it, petroleum reserves. No, wait, *relationships*!

So now I'm living a life of financial responsibility and gambling on risks worth taking, I'm married to and working with the most beautiful woman I've ever known, and I've seen a dozen book projects come to fruition under my watch, including our first book together

(*Marriable: Taking the Desperate Out of Dating*), and we have four more collaborations in the works.

I'm still working my tail off, all the while fighting the demons of procrastination, fear, and doubt that others have told me is not my battle alone. I believe the only redeeming value in making mistakes in life is being able to share what you've learned with others openly, without fear of rejection. That's how I knew I had to write this book. What bold undertaking are your demons afraid of?

Your Turn to Deal

If you just got out of jail, what's the first thing you would do?

Why are most people generally afraid to talk about their failures or the skeletons in their closet?

Can you think of anyone who has been to jail and turned his or her life around afterwards? Someone who hasn't? Why the difference?

THE WALK
OF FAME
AND THE
WALK OF
SHAME

He who observes the wind will not sow,
and he who regards the clouds will not reap.

Ecclesiastes 11:4 English Standard Version

All In translation:
If you wait for a life free of risk,
you'll never plant or harvest your dreams.

Most gamblers revel in the walk into the casino—the adrenaline, the palpable excitement. I used to call this the Walk of Fame. Even if I was fearful in the pit of my stomach, my exterior oozed confidence and my stride showed I was willing to risk. If you're a regular, everyone greets you by name, the waitresses know your favorite drink, and the pit boss offers to buy your meal come dinnertime—all to the wonderment of the casual gambler sitting next to you.

But most often for someone with a gambling problem, the walk out of the casino is one of trying not to be noticed. You hope no one noticed you going back to the ATM to play your "lucky four" keno/PIN numbers four different times, only to have reached your withdrawal limit for the day. You hope no one sees through your facade and sees you're hurting from more than your last bet. I called this the Walk of Shame.

Life outside the casino is no different.

How will you walk away from situations that require risk? Triumphant and cocky, thinking you can duplicate and deserve that result every time? Happy with the results but humble knowing that you are doing better than you deserve? Completely broke, with your head hung low searching for loose change to tip the valet? Briefly disappointed but confident in the fact that you haven't done anything immoral and are absent of fear except for the love of God and others?

Being able to visualize how you want to leave your life before the time comes will help you make decisions based on sure things versus long shots. You can't change the rules or odds of the game; the only two things you can change are your decisions and how you live with them.

Today you are faced with a choice, and as you know by now, choice involves risk. Are you willing to take inventory of your fears and the dangers associated with living life for the right reasons? Are you willing to live a life absent of all fear?

Make the following commitments with me now:

When confronted with risk in my life, I will no longer look to avoid risk for the sake of avoiding it.

I accept that risk is unavoidable and that by trying to avoid risk, I risk something different and potentially more negative in return.

God created me to be devoid of fear, and I entrust myself wholly to his hands to balance my life.

I accept that just like God and his Son Jesus were rejected, I too will experience rejection and should not be surprised or offended.

To fear the unavoidable is a waste of time; therefore, I refuse to fear rejection, old age, or death.

To love God with all your heart you must know him, and I commit to knowing him through studying his Word.

To love others as myself, I will temper my apple-induced,
self-centered motivation and seek to make my
motivations God-centered.

Making a commitment to follow through on these statements and repeatedly working on the "Your Turn to Deal" sections will catapult you into experiencing a healthy and exciting life of embracing risk, ignoring fear, and living life *All In.*

Michael DiMarco is CEO of Hungry Planet, a publishing company founded by his wife, Hayley, that works with fresh authors who want to reach an increasingly postmodern culture with premodern truth. Before helping manage Hungry Planet projects like *Mean Girls*, *The Gospel Unplugged*, and *Marriable*, Michael worked in publisher relations for an electronic publishing company, was a national speaker at pastors' and Christian conferences, coached volleyball for seven years at the university level, wrote award-winning humor columns on relationships, worked in talk radio, and cohosted a relationship humor radio show called *Babble of the Sexes*. Michael, Hayley, and their daughter, Addison, live in Nashville, Tennessee.

Hungry Planet is an independent publishing imprint and communications company that feeds the world's appetite for truth. Hungry Planet helps organizations understand and reach the multitasking assimilator mind-set, while Hungry Planet books tackle life's everyday issues with a distinctly modern spiritual voice. Visit Hungry Planet at www.hungryplanet.net.

"Feeding the World's Appetite for Truth"

What makes Hungry Planet books different?
Every Hungry Planet book attacks the senses of the reader with a postmodern mind-set (both visually and mentally) in a way unlike most books in the marketplace. Attention to every detail from physical appearance (book size, titling, cover, and interior design) to message (content and author's voice) helps Hungry Planet books connect with the more "visual" reader in ways that ordinary books can't.

With writing and packaging content for the young adult and "hip adult" markets, Hungry Planet books combine cutting-edge design with felt-need topics, all the while injecting a much-needed spiritual voice.

Why are publishers so eager to work with Hungry Planet?
Because of the innovative success and profitable track record of HP projects from the bestselling *Dateable* and *Mean Girls* to the Gold Medallion–nominated *The Dirt on Sex* (part of HP's The Dirt series). Publishers also take notice of HP founder Hayley (Morgan) DiMarco's past success in creating big ideas like the "Biblezine" concept while she was brand manager for Thomas Nelson Publishers' teen book division.

How does Hungry Planet come up with such big ideas?
Hayley and HP general manager/husband Michael DiMarco tend to create their best ideas at mealtime, which in the DiMarco household is around five times a day. Once the big idea and scope of the topic is established, the couple decides either to write the content themselves or find an up-and-coming author with a passion for the topic. HP then partners with a publisher to create the book.

How do I find out more about Hungry Planet?
Use the web, silly—www.hungryplanet.net

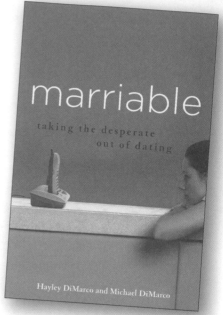

Coming Spring 2007

The Man Manual:
Mastering the Moves, Power-Ups, and
Pitfalls to Becoming a Real Man

ℜ Revell
www.revellbooks.com

Hungry Planet
www.hungryplanet.net

www.allinbook.com